# "Finally!

**GET WHAT YOU DESERVE!** is the right book for these insane times. Job security is...DEAD. We must ALL become effective self-marketers; and you simply won't find a better pair of guides than Jay Levinson and Seth Godin. LEARNED A LOT! Bravo!!"

## Tom Peters

author, *Thriving on Chaos* and *The Pursuit of Wow!*

# GET WHAT YOU DESERVE!

### How to Guerrilla Market Yourself

Jay Levinson
and
Seth Godin

AVON BOOKS  NEW YORK

AVON BOOKS
A division of
The Hearst Corporation
1350 Avenue of the Americas
New York, New York 10019

Library of Congress Cataloging in Publication Data:

Levinson, Jay Conrad.
Get what you deserve : how to guerrilla market yourself /
Jay Conrad Levinson and Seth Godin.
p.    cm.
Includes index.
1. Career development.  2. Self-presentation.  3. Success in business.
I. Godin, Seth.  II. Title.
HF5381.L3562  1997                              97-3149
650.14—dc21                                        CIP

First Avon Books Printing: September 1997

AVON TRADEMARK REG. U.S. PAT. OFF. AND IN OTHER COUNTRIES, MARCA REGISTRADA,
HECHO EN U.S.A.

Printed in the U.S.A.

FIRST EDITION

QPM     10  9  8  7  6  5  4  3  2  1

# From Jay

This book is dedicated to Mike Lavin, Dick Atwood, Randy Zucker, Bob Lipman, Don Bennett, Bill Stein, and Joel Coopersmith for getting what they deserve and giving me what I deserve for fifteen years in a row.

I gratefully acknowledge the help and inspiration given to me by my brilliant co-author, Seth Godin; my wife, Patsy; my daughter, Amy; my grandchildren, Sage, Seth, and Natty; my agents, Mike Larsen and Elizabeth Pomada; my jack-of-every-trade, Bill Shear; my webmeister, Bill Gallagher; and my bluegrass guerrilla, Candace Lynn Jones. May all of these people get what they deserve—the very best.

# From Seth

If you met a couple just like your parents at a cocktail party, would you stop and talk with them? Most people would run in the other direction. I'm lucky. My parents are intelligent, thoughtful, well-spoken, motivated, and a lot of fun. They are an inspiration and I owe them more than just a dedication—but here one is.

This book wouldn't have existed without the people who have taught me and those who have believed in the journey I've been on: Zig Ziglar, Lisa Gansky, Sam Attenberg, Michael Cader, Tom Cohen, Joanne Kates, Elly Markson, David Seuss, Bill Bowman, Steve Dennis, Barry Bronfin, Beth Emme, Doug Glen, Robert Leinwand, Lynn Gordon, Dan Lovy, and Steve Lewers.

It's been a dream come true to work with my guru, Jay Levinson, a visionary, a wise man, a scholar, a friend, and a mensch.

This book came to pass in my "spare time," thanks to the outstanding efforts of a small squadron of people who give heart and soul to support our mission. Special thanks to my muses, the gang of four: Karen Watts, Lisa DiMona, Robin Dellabough, and Julie Maner. Many thanks to Sarah Silbert, who edited beautifully, and to Anne Shepherd, who kept the roof from falling in. And a sincere tip of the hat to Amy Winger.

Our team at Avon Books—led by Lou Aronica and Lisa Considine—is outstanding. This book is in terrific hands.

Helene, Max, and Alex are the big reason for everything. Thanks.

*"What is a date really,
but a job interview that lasts all night?"*
—Jerry Seinfeld

*T*o *get what you deserve* . . .
Let people know how talented, motivated, and honest you are.


*T*o *let people know how talented, motivated, and honest you are* . . .
Market yourself.


Guerrilla Marketing Yourself is the science of persuading people that you deserve to succeed.

# Is This Book For You?

*If you're trying to get a job . . .*
This book will teach you how to put your best foot forward on paper and in an interview.

*If you do business by phone . . .*
The techniques in this book will dramatically increase your success.

*If you'd like to strengthen your marriage . . .*
This book will give you tools and strategies to make your relationship thrive.

*If you'd like to be treated with respect wherever you go . . .*
The simple secrets revealed here will empower you to get what you want and deserve.

*If you're trying to build more stable relationships . . .*
This book will show you how to diagnose what often goes wrong and how to avoid it.

*If you'd like to get promoted . . .*
This book will teach you to demonstrate just how good you are to your boss.

*If you'd like to sell something—anything . . .*
This book will explain exactly how to sell yourself first so that it is very easy for people to buy whatever else you are selling.

*If you'd like to feel you're getting everything you deserve . . .*
**Get What You Deserve!** will help you eliminate the hidden barriers to success.

# CONTENTS

# GET WHAT
# YOU DESERVE!

## INTRODUCTION

# *Why You Should Bother Spending the Time*

◆

LAST YEAR, MORE THAN 10 MILLION SELF-HELP BOOKS WERE sold. An awful lot of them were bought by people with the best intentions, but the readers never followed through and implemented the ideas. Even worse, some of these books were never read.

That's not surprising. Changing your life for the better isn't easy, or everyone would do it! All too often, these books outline wonderful plans but never answer the question, "What's in it for me?" Why bother spending the time, the energy, and the resources to follow the author's advice?

This book has an audacious title. You'd all like to get what you deserve, and we believe that this book can dramatically increase the chances for your success. You're probably wondering a few things about our guerrilla marketing concept.

"Does it really work?"

"Is it hard?"

"How long will it take to get results?"

"Why should I invest the time and energy to do things that make me a little uncomfortable, or make me feel unnatural?"

Because it will transform your life. Because it will change the way the world treats you. Because it will make you happier.

There are two keys to success—knowing what you want and knowing how to get it. *Get What You Deserve!* will help you figure out what you want, but more important, it will provide you with the tools and the mind-set you'll need to succeed.

In a nutshell, this book asks and answers crucial questions:

➤ What messages do you send?
➤ How do you send them?
➤ Who do you send them to?
➤ What messages do you want to send?

Finding the answers to these questions will equip you to reexamine the way you relate to the world and what effect it has on how the world treats you.

This book won't suggest you tell people what they want to hear, but it explains how to tell them what you want them to hear. It will show you a new way of thinking about how you interact with the world that will enable you to figure out what you want and how to get it more effectively.

This is not a book about being someone you're not. It's not going to tell you how to persuade someone to hire you as president when you're really qualified to be an assistant. What it is going to do is demonstrate how to represent your qualities and skills so you never get less than you deserve.

The system described here works. It works for individuals, for organizations, and for businesses. Over the last fifteen years, we have counseled literally thousands of executives, salespeople, and "people on the street" on how to use guerrilla techniques to find success. Now those secrets are available to you.

Unlike other self-help books, we don't want you to change who you are. Your basic nature is just fine the way it is. This is a book about changing how you act, how you convey your image, how you send signals.

Sometimes we're lucky enough to find a pattern that translates into success. Like Mary did. When Mary finally made it to college, she was determined to be a success. Her goal was to have a position at a top law firm by the time she was thirty. She knew that was a tall order, and she was willing to work. But more than that, she was eager and excited to be where she was.

And she talked to everyone. She introduced herself to her professors, to her classmates, and even to some administrators when she encountered them. Her motivation showed through in each conversation, and she was open, friendly, and confident, which made everyone she talked to feel at ease.

Mary quickly realized what a powerful tool this was. She was making friends like crazy, and her professors were responsive to her ideas and seemed to think well of her. Soon she had made a strong enough impression through her popularity and good reputation that professors she'd never met before seemed to respect her and her work readily.

Ever since Mary had been a freshman in college, she had had no trouble getting her way. She had won every election, had got every job, had received every promotion. How? Not by being the smartest person in the room and not by working the hardest. After her experience in school, she knew what she had to do—whether it was the head of the board of trustees or the senior rainmaker at her law firm—Mary managed to introduce herself to the right people and quickly gain their trust. To others it sometimes feels as if Mary went to school with, served on a board with, or is related to just about everyone she meets.

Since she's a stranger to no one, life's a lot easier for Mary. She's trusted, respected, and welcomed. Her ideas get the benefit of the doubt. She's the first person people call when they need someone to sit on an important committee or give a welcoming speech.

*　　*　　*

Scott is a minor celebrity. His work as a computer programmer has been featured in a number of industry magazines, and the perception among opinion leaders is that he's one of the select few in his field who's a "genius." But Scott's no genius. He's just a hardworking programmer who knows how to focus his efforts on the right problems.

Because he's surrounded by an aura of success, Scott has more freelance business than he can handle. And because other programmers respect his skills, he spends precious little time persuading others to abandon their ideas and embrace his. In short, he's turned his reputation into a tool for efficiency.

*　　*　　*

Why does everyone want to date Laura? She's no supermodel, and she's not rich. She has an interesting job at MTV, though, and the zeal that got her there is apparent in her approach to each person she meets and every project she starts. With her enthusiastic handshake and genuine smile, you can just tell that she's fun to be around.

Laura hasn't been lonely in a long time. And she doesn't expect to be lonely anytime soon.

\* \* \*

Chris is a computer executive who's on his third job in six years. Each position has turned out very well, and the latest led to a call from an executive recruiter, a 60 percent boost in salary, and a new promotion. Last year, Chris earned $240,000. And he's just twenty-nine years old.

How does Chris, who's really sort of an average guy, manage to turn above-average performance into a string of better and better jobs?

He's learned how to focus his energy and efforts on the people and the projects that matter. Without aggressively overselling himself, Chris has managed to identify exactly what his employers and future employers want from him. And he delivers it.

\* \* \*

Susan and Bill have a fantastic marriage. Every year, they fall more in love with each other. While other couples complain that the magic is gone, that they're stuck in a rut, Susan and Bill find themselves enjoying their time together more and more.

Bill points to a day ten years ago when he and Susan almost got divorced. They were talking *at* each other instead of *to* each other. They had confused expectations about what they were trying to accomplish and their marriage was almost ruined.

Then Bill realized they were taking each other for granted. He and Susan were no longer paying attention to the tone of voice they used with each other, or how they spent their time together. Without meaning to, they were telling each other: "I don't care about you." They learned to be more aware of these things and they consciously stopped sending that message. The hurt feelings it once caused no longer stood in the way of their communication.

Instead of each focusing inward from moment to moment, they focused on their goals for the relationship and how to deliver what the other was looking for. By making the effort to smile after a really bad day, Bill told Susan: "I'm happy to see you and I care more about you than a hard day at work." By reexamining what their current behavior was transmitting to each other, figuring out what it was they wanted to say, and finding patterns of communication that worked, they rebuilt their foundation, and their relationship grew and began to thrive once again.

This simple adjustment in their approach changed everything. They both ended up getting exactly what they needed from the relationship, but they did it by marketing, not by demanding.

The world is filled with success stories. People who started with nothing: no money, no connections, no extraordinary god-given talents. They turned nothing into happiness, friendships, respect, and even fame and money. How?

We're going to tell you. These ideas will transform your life if you let them. There are no big secrets here. Nothing that's been stored in a black book in a monastery for centuries. These are proven principles that are guaranteed to get results if you implement them.

Guerrilla marketing works. It's worked for thousands and thousands of people around the world. Now it's your turn. Take a chance, use these tools, invest in yourself, and then watch the world change around you.

## Seth and Jay's Guerrilla Marketing Histories

Before we get started, we thought you might like to know a little about where the ideas in this book came from. We very much practice what we preach, and everything you'll read about is directly related to our personal experience.

## Seth's Guerrilla Marketing History

I became a guerrilla marketer at fourteen, when I started my first business. If you don't know what a guerrilla or a marketer is, don't worry. Neither did I. Instead, I just followed my entrepreneurial instincts. Running small businesses became a habit, and without knowing it, I began practicing many of the precepts of Jay's yet unwritten guerrilla marketing books.

In college, I ran the largest student-run business in the country. We had a snack bar, a ticket agency, temporary employment and laundry services, and even a travel agency. My partner and I started a new "division" every week or so and had a fantastic time discovering how small businesses worked.

After going to Stanford, where I set a record for missing as many classes as possible and still collecting an MBA, I became a brand manager at a software company. If you don't know what a brand manager does, don't worry— neither did I at first. It was there I met Jay and first came to understand that there was a method to guerrilla marketing. Suddenly, the techniques I had been using accidentally made sense, and I began a focused program to put them into practice.

Jay's original guerrilla marketing book was a breakthrough. It quickly became a classic because of the original way it redefined what marketing a business was all about. By focusing on the small things—the individuals who buy a product and what makes them decide on one product over another—Jay completely reinvented the modern art of marketing.

I used Jay's techniques to build a multimillion-dollar brand at Spinnaker. Our products were in every relevant store, and we appeared in everything from *Rolling Stone* to *The Wall Street Journal* to *Playboy*.

However, it quickly became clear that there was a difference between marketing a business and marketing myself. Time and time again, I discovered that my ideas weren't as well received as I had hoped, even though I knew they were well conceived. I also realized that I didn't have as many friends as I wanted.

When *InfoWorld* magazine wrote about my company, they had a brief paragraph about me, the twenty-four-year-old marketing whiz kid. They called me "brash." At the time, I didn't really understand that comment. In retrospect, it makes perfect sense. I was putting people off.

While there were people who were willing to work with me, there were others who decided it wasn't worth the trouble. For example, because I wasn't projecting the right message, my boss avoided me at every opportunity. At one point, he went without speaking to me for a month. Talk about a career-limiting move! Because of the way I marketed myself, the way I presented my ideas, the speed with which I worked, I was a threat to him. He tried to get me fired but failed, and decided instead to just deal with me as little as possible.

I moved to New York and started my own company, inventing and selling book ideas to publishers. In the first year, I received nine hundred rejection letters. My wife and I used to window-shop at restaurants, and I was as close to giving up as I'd ever been.

That's when I had my marketing epiphany. And just in time.

I had been walking into meetings with publishers as a

hotshot marketing wizard with a fancy suit and an MBA. I presented them with statistical analyses and focus group data. I was arrogant. I knew I was right.

You know what? It didn't matter. Being right doesn't make you rich. Being right doesn't make you successful. I may have had profitable concepts, but the personality I was projecting to the publishers I met with was all wrong. I was too corporate, too young, too quick.

That doesn't mean that being a hotshot marketing wizard with a fancy suit and an MBA never works. In a lot of industries it works just fine. But I was being internally inconsistent. I was selling a "product" that my customers didn't want to buy.

Finally, as a last resort, I decided to try a different tack. I found someone in my field who was successful and modeled myself after him—his approach, his behavior, his attitude. Instead of creating laser-printed desktop-published proposals, I typed them. Instead of faxing or overnighting all my documents, I mailed them. Instead of wearing a suit and tie, I wore a sport coat or a sweater.

Within three weeks, I sold a book. Within a year, five books. Within two years, I had sold more than twenty books. In large part, this turnaround came from sending a message that was more palatable to the people I was dealing with. It came from marketing myself.

I wasn't being insincere. I was delighted to scale back the MBA shtick and focus on the relationships and the content. It made my job more fun. And even better, it matched expectations and it worked.

Surprisingly, the incredible implications of this turnaround didn't hit me right away. As I discovered new industries and met new people, I didn't spend much time thinking about how and why I was judging people and people were judging me. I got much better at presenting myself and my ideas and was able to increase the size and profitability of my business. But I never spent very much time analyzing how I was doing it.

The growth of my company, though, has really changed my thinking. We've taken out full-page ads in *The New York Times* looking for employees, and I've probably interviewed a thousand people for jobs, and I'm amazed at what I see. From résumés to cover letters to outfits to interview techniques to handshakes—people sabotage themselves at every turn.

There was a writer who came in unshaven and in a ripped motorcycle jacket. An editor who interrupted every question. A candidate we never met who responded to our lack of interest with a threat of a lawsuit for discrimination— and, at the same time, a plea for freelance work.

Am I drawing conclusions about these people too quickly? With a thousand interviews over a few years, if I spent enough time to get to know everyone, I'd never get any work done. There's a lot going on in my life, and I'm the first to admit that I grasp at clues to figure out what makes someone tick. And you know what? Everyone does.

I wanted to shake some of these self-sabotaging people, especially the apparently qualified ones. "Make eye contact!" I wanted to yell. "Quit blaming your last boss for everything!" It sometimes seemed like I was witnessing a new TV show: *How to Get Rejected.*

Once we grew to ten employees, I started to have a chance to see people operating in the workplace. Employees market themselves from the moment they walk in the door to the moment they leave at night. There's the cranky editor who sends nasty e-mail about her boss to other employees. The hardworking, flexible associate, who must know that marketing herself in that way will lead to more success later. From the minute they arrive at work, people market themselves to their boss and their coworkers—and everyone can see if they're inconsistent.

People would like you to believe that they're always consistent, that they market themselves the same to everyone they meet. But since I've started watching people, I've noticed the difference between the way employees present themselves to fellow employees and others they interact with as opposed to how they approach the outside world. As I entered other work environments, it was fascinating to see people who are at peace with their fellow workers treat an outsider like a criminal. Lawyers who would yell at a secretary and kiss up to a client.

As I realized the power that guerrilla marketing yourself could bring, I worked hard to implement it in my life. At home, I am an energetic, considerate, thoughtful spouse, though I probably worry too much about money. My kids see me as a leader: a strict, consistent, superfun dad who's never too busy to play, and who's always bringing home a comic book or an electric screwdriver.

At work, I'm hardworking, accessible to my employees, flexible on some issues, and a stickler on others. Some people call me driven, and I'm sort of proud of that. I've been extremely demanding to employees on personal development and quality, and very supportive at the same time. I consistently send a message that work has to be in balance with personal life. One employee called our office the healthiest place she's ever worked.

As a company, we've shown ourselves to be out-of-the-box thinkers who will go the extra mile to help a client with a marketing problem. There are companies that wait to be told what to do, but we position ourselves as a company that solves problems. We're not screamers, nor are we cheaters. We're not mad scientists out of touch with reality either. Instead, our clients find a reliable, stable source of really cool ideas.

My professional image is that of a slightly off-the-wall marketing guru, someone who will tweak convention by ordering jumpsuits for the staff (navy surplus, export to Iraq prohibited), but will also have a spreadsheet ready to support a new business idea. I'm trying to be consistent, quality-conscious, fast, insightful, and clever, and working to express all of these qualities to people I work with.

How much of who I've become occurred naturally and how much was consciously decided? It's no longer possible to separate the two aspects of my life. By identifying my goals in personal marketing, and living toward them, I've become what I hoped to be. I'm not likely to sue someone or to yell at someone or to take a shortcut on an ethical call. It's not something my intentional self even thinks about anymore. Even if I wanted to spend a day at work daydreaming and playing air hockey, it's not likely. The driven part of me won't allow it.

What you'll find in this book is a blueprint for how I turned the insight about marketing myself into a solid program. Jay set the foundation for this thinking with his first book and with all the books since then—the ones he has done with us as well as those with others. More important, he's set it with his own example. Let him tell you.

### Jay's Guerrilla Marketing History

I didn't know thing one about guerrillas or marketing when I was discharged from the U.S. Army. All I knew was that I loved to write and that I didn't want to work for a newspaper. When I was a member of the army's counterintelligence corps, even though the cloak-and-dagger part was fun, I found writing the reports of my investigations was even better.

So I tried to get a job as a writer in an advertising agency. Presenting myself as a writer sure didn't work because I had zero advertising experience. To get a job in an ad agency meant I had to market myself as what I really and truly was—an incredibly fast typist who was willing to learn shorthand, to wash floors and windows, and to run every demeaning errand anyone needed. I was hired as a secretary at $75.00 per week. And I was thrilled.

I spent each day, from nine to five, being a dutiful secretary and acting the part. Nobody at that agency was better at fetching coffee and hot chocolate. After five, I became a copywriter, taking on assignments that had been given to my boss and putting them on his desk. Each morning, I'd arrive to see that my copy had been blue-penciled to death. But I'd try again. And again. Finally, my boss, impressed by my persistence and the quality of the copy I'd produced, allowed the copy I had written to be published. And he promoted me to copywriter. No raise. But I was allowed to have business cards. They were my first ever and they gave me a sense of my own identity. After all, here I was being identified in print as a real, honest-to-goodness copywriter.

Even though I had been promoted, I was still viewed as a onetime secretary so I sought another job where they'd think of me as a copywriter. I marketed myself as a tireless, high-energy copywriter, a quick learner who had a lot to learn and was eager to write anything and meet any deadline. I also made it clear that while I worked hard, I went home at five, didn't take work home, and never worked on weekends.

I was working alongside people who had very different

positions. There was the copywriter who was slow but worked every single weekend and kept his job through sheer will. The copywriter who intimidated everyone into thinking his copy must be good. He didn't last as long.

My approach served me well as I went from ad agency to ad agency—in San Francisco, Chicago, London, and back to Chicago. Each time, I got a better job. Each job leaned heavily upon my writing ability and ability to make even the most unreasonable deadlines without complaining. Each job was a pure joy to me. I marketed myself by focusing on the elements of my work ethic that were a dream come true to the agency that hired me.

My years in London were during the Beatles heyday, and when I returned to the States, I had longer hair than most guys and dressed far more informally. I wasn't really thinking in terms of marketing myself, what my attire and hair length would mean to my career, or what anyone would think about it. Until once, when I went to New York to make a presentation to a Fortune 500 company, everybody stared at my ponytail as I presented. "Uh-oh," I thought. "These people are judging me by my hair and not by my work!" Could I have made it farther up the corporate ladder by marketing myself as more corporate? Probably. But I made a choice and stuck with it.

Standing on a street corner during a bitter cold February day in Chicago, I decided that as much as I loved the White Sox, Chicago was not the place for me. So my wife, daughter, and I moved to San Francisco, where I planned to seek employment with a different advertising agency.

While job hunting, I did freelance writing and immediately realized that without meetings and memos, people coming into my office to shoot the breeze, and me putting out fires, I was able to complete in three days what used to take me five. And I decided to run my own business from my own home. That was in 1971 and I haven't looked back since.

All this time, I continued to highlight my strengths: I was still a fast typist, still able to meet even the most draconian deadlines, and still head over heels in love with writing. I continued to dress informally but that actually helped, becaused it stressed that hiring the freelancer without a suit got you better copy, not a better wardrobe.

Instead of trying to market myself to many, I pinpointed the top companies and agencies in the San Francisco Bay Area. I wrote directed letters and mailed them individually. When I'd meet with a prospective client, I would wear a tie (I didn't even own a fancy suit), but I'd market my talents and abilities, my experience and my past clients—not my attire. The rough edges were a plus, especially in San Francisco.

I began writing books in 1973. Actually, it was on a Saturday morning in 1973 when I wrote my first book, self-published it, and got my feet wet as an author. That led to more books and those led to speaking engagements. Because I spoke to business audiences, I wore a tie. But when my total book sales surpassed the one million mark, I discarded the tie, began wearing my trademark white slip-on sneakers, and wore designer jeans with my blue blazer when I spoke. Comfort above all. But it wasn't just comfort. It was marketing. Corporate audiences were used to fancy suits and fancy ties and fancy haircuts. I didn't have any of that. So what I was saying must have been important. I stood out.

When I worked at the ad agency, I'm sure my unconventional attire and decor surprised many of my coworkers, but since I was a member of a creative team, they would just chalk it up to "weird behavior by one of those creative hotshots."

Being seen as a creative was a plus then, and it's a plus now. For me.

Today, I market myself almost exactly as I did when I first started. I'm still a fast typist, now faster than ever. I still love like crazy to write. I still love to learn. I'm still very informal in business matters. I still meet deadlines, still rarely work after five.

I consider myself blessed beyond belief to get to be myself and to have now taken on the aura of an "author" who has written twenty-three books. I think more about what I offer than what I am—information that will help entrepreneurs and would-be entrepreneurs to achieve freedom and balance, profitability, and joy in their work.

This enthusiasm for my work obviously colors my own identity, and people think of me as a "guerrilla guru," which is hardly the way I think of myself. I think of myself as a guy who is nuts about writing and lucky enough to be able to do what he loves and work from his own home. But the positioning as a guerrilla guru is important for those who buy my books and attend my lectures, and I indulge it.

I've been married for over 40 years to the same woman and my marketing to her is something I'm able to deliver on: honest, enthusiastic, and hardworking. She didn't marry me for my biceps or sartorial splendor. I consistently deliver her a caring, sensitive, connected husband, and I think she appreciates it!

I am unbelievably fortunate to have been able to earn a living and to make a life doing exactly what I like to do. I am able to daydream, to play air hockey, to watch White Sox games on my satellite dish, and sometimes to go to sleep content that I have accomplished absolutely nothing that day. I have learned that if I am true to myself, everything else seems to fall into place. I offer that same advice to you—if your dreams are consistent with the marketing tactics you're willing to engage in, you're bound for success. The good news is that you get to decide the tradeoffs in advance and market yourself to get what you deserve.

Before you get started, take this quiz. Respond to each statement as you see yourself, not as you think others see you:

TRUE OR FALSE
1. I am trustworthy and honest.
2. I am an open, friendly person.
3. I am intelligent and well-spoken.
4. I am a hard worker.
5. I am a reliable friend.
6. I am funny and pleasant to be around.
7. I have confidence in myself.
8. I want the people around me to be happy and comfortable.
9. I am ambitious and goal-oriented.
10. I care what other people think of me.

How did you do? If you're like most people, you responded to most with True. You *do* see yourself as honest, hardworking, friendly, ambitious, funny, pleasant, reliable, and more. But does everyone else? Think about it this way:

TRUE OR FALSE
The last person who rejected me—who fired me, turned me down, or broke up with me—probably didn't think that:

1. I am trustworthy and honest.
2. I am an open, friendly person.
3. I am intelligent and well-spoken.
4. I am a hard worker.

5. I am a reliable friend.
6. I am funny and pleasant to be around.
7. I have confidence in myself.
8. I want the people around me to be happy and comfortable.
9. I am ambitious and goal-oriented.
10. I care what other people think of me.

There is one basic step that separates these two quizzes—communication. If what you think of yourself differs from what others think of you, you are not expressing yourself effectively to those around you, and the lack of communication is leading to rejection. But no more. This book will teach you the skills you need to make sure everyone around you knows how talented, friendly, trustworthy, and capable you really are. Follow the simple guidelines outlined in these chapters and you'll be able to stop the cycle of rejections caused by misunderstandings or miscommunications. This book will show you how to take control—and get what you deserve!

## About This Book

This book is a journey. We want to take you through twenty years of thinking, experiments, and results, and show you how guerrilla marketing techniques can change every element of your life.

First, we need to demonstrate how vitally important it is that you market yourself at all. Then, we'll help you understand marketing and what distinguishes a guerrilla marketer from an ordinary marketer. This distinction will make the difference between a general, hit-and-miss marketing campaign and the focused, comprehensive road to success.

We'll offer our personal experiences to show how applicable and effective these forces are in everyday life. You'll see that neither of our stories are unbelievable—no overnight millions, no instant fame. These are simple techniques that rely more on consistency and persistence than brilliance or luck.

Then, we'll let you in on the Golden Secret of the guerrilla marketer. Once you understand and believe this, your interactions will never be the same.

In the next chapter, we're going to help you figure out what you want. Easy, right? A good job, to be well-liked, plenty of money. But sometimes some of the things we want make it impossible to get others. We'll show you why this is, and how to figure out what your real goals are.

When a friend describes you, what does he or she say? Surprised this is marketing? This book will show you how many roles marketing plays in your life without you even thinking about it. Then by showing you how product marketing works, we'll demonstrate how important it is that you market yourself.

The following chapter will reveal what impact all the things you do, wear, say, and express have on your success or failure every day. We'll help you get a sense of what you're communicating about yourself, and how different that is from what you want others to understand about you. Then we'll help you figure out how to reconcile the two. God is in the details, and so is marketing. Everything you do sends a signal, and we'll show you some concrete examples.

Then we'll give you the definitive Twelve Rules of Guerrilla Marketing and the Guerrilla Marketing Credo, which will be the base of, and strength behind, your personal marketing campaign. With these principles, you can figure out how to market yourself in virtually any situation, maximizing the odds that you'll get what you deserve.

All the stories in this book are true. In most cases, names are changed to respect the privacy of the individuals mentioned. A note about ethnocentrism: We believe that the concepts and techniques discussed herein are universal, but the examples we give come from our own experience, which is certainly not universal.

### WARNING!

The tools described in this book are very powerful. They will allow you to market yourself more effectively to almost anyone. They will give you the ability to meet more people, have successful job interviews, sell more products or services, make friends, and impress strangers.

If you use these strategies to better market the skills and attributes you have, you'll find that they lead to unimagined achievement. However, if you use them to manipulate, to portray yourself as someone you aren't and can't become, you'll be disappointed. You'll discover that great marketing isn't much without a great product, and you'll be bound for failure.

We're confident that you have the attitude, the skills, the goals, and most important, the honesty needed to go all the way to the top. This book can show you how to market yourself so that you get there.

# CHAPTER ONE
## *People Judge You*

———————◆———————

JIM WAS COMING BACK FROM A VACATION IN MEXICO. HE WAS a respected teacher and a camp director, entrusted with the lives of hundreds of kids every summer. Few people who knew him could name someone more reliable, more serious about his work, more middle-of-the-road.

Unfortunately, the customs officer in Chicago didn't know any of these people. All he knew was that Jim had long hair and was wearing a dirty tee-shirt. Of the several hundred people switching planes that day at O'Hare, the undercover officer decided that Jim was a suspect.

Approaching him, he flashed a badge and took him aside. Jim was strip-searched, his baggage taken apart inch by inch. Somewhat chagrined, the inspectors found nothing, not even an undeclared postcard. They held his plane for him on the runway and drove him out to meet it.

Despite the apologies of the agents, Jim was understandably upset. When he thought about the incident later, though, he realized that they were just doing a job. If anything, it was his fault. The way he dressed, the way he wore his hair—he was sending a signal.

The customs agents had an assignment. Using very little information, they were supposed to judge people, to separate the likely smugglers from those less likely to break the law. Given the way Jim was marketing himself, they jumped to a defensible conclusion.

When you think about it, isn't the Miss America Pageant a bit odd? After all, the sight of fifty college-educated women, wearing high heels and bathing suits, is a little silly. Add to this the ballet, baton twirling, and piano playing, and you've created a competition that hardly seems designed to select America's outstanding woman.

The pageant uses eight judges, none of whom have ever met these fifty women, to winnow the group quickly to ten semifinalists, then five finalists, then just one winner. The judges do this in just a few hours, using nothing but very superficial criteria.

But really, your life is a lot like the Miss America Pageant. Every day you're in front of a panel of judges, people you don't know, who form opinions about you. The difference is that the Miss America Pageant is fairer. At least the judges admit that they're evaluating people. At least the losers realize that it's just a pageant, not a final grade on their worth as human beings. You interact with judges all the time. Job interviewers. Your boss. Prospective customers. Potential investors. New friends. The maître d' at a fancy restaurant. A cop giving you a ticket. The kid taking your order at McDonald's. They judge the way you look, the way you talk, the way you act. They measure your actions, your inactions, and your reputation. Every day, everyone you deal with is judging you.

It's not just your appearance, either. It's the way you conduct a meeting, the conversation you have with a longtime friend on the telephone, the house you live in, just about everything you say or do.

And while these people are busy observing you and making their assumptions, you're doing it right back at them.

## Strangers

Your boss asked you to work late tonight. Leaving about ten, you start walking down the street to get your car. Suddenly, you hear footsteps behind you. Looking back, you see two strangers, a couple of rattily dressed teenagers, walking behind you.

Do you walk a little faster? Does your heart start beating a little louder?

What if the shadowy-looking strangers were two old friends? Or two policemen in uniform? Or perhaps two people, one of whom had found the wallet you had dropped.

We're scared of strangers, aren't we?

Where does that fear come from? Well, for starters, your great-great-grandparents lived a different life from yours.

It wasn't just the lack of computers, telephones, television sets, and fax machines. The world was a different place 150 years ago. Most of the population lived in small villages, and travel was rare. If you went somewhere, you walked, unless you were lucky enough to have a horse.

For thousands and thousands of years, humans lived in villages like these. Generation after generation lived in exactly the same circumstances. Agrarian-based, the village was the center of their lives.

The most important attribute of a village was that strangers were rare or even unheard of. People spent their entire lives living with people they knew.

Over many generations, people came to fear strangers.

After all, they were ill-equipped to determine whether a stranger meant them harm or not, since they had spent their lives with people they'd known since birth.

It's important not to underestimate the impact this living arrangement had on our culture. Our heritage is not based on diverse populations, changing environments, and constant evolution of ideas and concepts. Most of our culture, our heritage, is based on a static village, a place where everything is knowable.

The depth of this apprehension is evident from children's stories and nursery rhymes. Strangers represent evil, something to fear.

## Too Many People

Make a list of some of the people you interacted with yesterday for the first time. Waitresses, coworkers, deliverymen, people on the elevator, salesmen on the phone, political candidates on the street. If you suffered from agoraphobia, imagine the discomfort of a trip to the mall. You would speak with a dozen salespeople (some on commission), sit in the food court with hundreds of strangers, and perhaps even watch a parking attendant—another stranger—drive your car away.

How is it possible to make the cultural transition from living an entire life with one hundred family members and friends to the high-speed, high-transaction life we live today? Always adaptable, our culture and our approach to strangers has changed dramatically.

We don't focus so much on getting to know people anymore. According to one study, it's unlikely that anyone has more than a dozen really close relationships. Instead, we've become experts at separating enemies from friends, masters at identifying danger and finding people we can trust.

Even if you wanted to be more thoughtful in the way you evaluate people, you wouldn't have time—you know *too many people*.

Take a look at this list of famous people:

| | |
|---|---|
| George Bush | Boris Yeltsin |
| George Jetson | Vladimir Lenin |
| Mark Twain | John Lennon |
| Bill Gates | Paul McCartney |
| Darryl Gates | Stevie Wonder |
| Nelson Rockefeller | The Maytag Repairman |
| Spiro Agnew | Snap, Crackle, and Pop |
| Beavis | Max Headroom |
| Butt-Head | Neil Armstrong |
| Marge Simpson | General George Custer |
| Buckaroo Banzai | Benedict Arnold |
| Andre Agassi | Paul Revere |
| Winston Churchill | Booker T |
| Moses | Mr. T |
| Andy Rooney | Joe DiMaggio |
| Ann Landers | Ted Koppel |
| Mikhail Baryshnikov | Stephen King |
| Michael Jordan | Fran Tarkenton |
| The Brothers Karamazov | Luciano Pavarotti |

How many of these people are you familiar with? Most people can identify more than 100,000 faces! Given this list, how many would you say you know? Even if you don't know them, no doubt you feel you can describe them pretty well. How is that possible? As we've developed our people-reading antennae, we've mastered countless shortcuts because there just isn't enough time in the day to learn everything about everyone. Was Winston Churchill a good father? Can

Andre Agassi spell? What's it like to play golf with George Bush? There's no way you can take the time to know all the people you recognize.

Some of these shortcuts are incredibly useful: "Don't buy stock from someone who calls on the phone during dinner." And some of them are damaging our society: "Teenagers are likely to shoplift." Some people call these shortcuts prejudice. In many ways they are—we're judging people without knowing whether the judgment is true in each particular case.

While prejudice is usually used to describe racial or religious judgment, we couldn't survive without the many stereotypes that have evolved—we need the shortcuts that come from prejudices to make quick decisions. Prejudices help us evaluate people when we don't have enough time to discover the truth on our own.

When Thomas Dewey ran against Harry Truman for President, famed bettor Jimmy "The Greek" Snyder bet $170,000 that Truman would win. How could he do this? Dewey was favored in all the polls, wasn't he? He sure was, but Jimmy knew that Dewey had a mustache and that most people in the United States trust nonmustached Presidential candidates more than those who sport mustaches. Truman, of course, won. And no President since the turn of the century has had a mustache.

Here are some examples of shortcuts you may have taken—or been victim of:

> ➤ Blond women aren't as smart as brunettes.
> ➤ Well-dressed white men aren't muggers.
> ➤ Famous people are trustworthy.
> ➤ People who don't dress well don't have much money.
> ➤ Salesmen can't be trusted.

➤ Confident people know what they're doing.

➤ Women who have flat tires need help more than men.

➤ Someone in a uniform can be trusted.

➤ People who don't speak English well aren't very smart.

➤ Harvard graduates are motivated and smarter than average.

➤ People with British accents are sophisticated.

Each of the statements, when stated as a rule, is clearly untrue. Yet many people, when forced to make a decision in a hurry, rely on these and hundreds of other "laws" to make significant decisions.

Of course, most of the opinions we form aren't as extreme as the ones we've just listed. We decide whether to trust someone based on thousands of subtle clues, clues that we'll describe throughout this book.

Tricia is an old friend. You've known her for more than a decade and join her family for parties, dinners, and holidays. She's a successful photographer and takes pictures of celebrities on location all over the world. Last night, at a swanky restaurant, she announced that she's going to school to train to become a minister. "That's quite a career change," you say. "Not really. Not if you knew me well." Momentarily chagrined, you realize that with just a few exceptions, you never know anyone very well.

We pigeonhole most people. We find the fewest number of words and attributes necessary to remember a person's distinctive character and then file it away. Teddy Roosevelt was an outdoorsman. George Washington chopped down a cherry tree. Abraham Lincoln freed the slaves. Gerald Ford kept falling down. Richard Nixon was a crook.

We all do it. All the people we meet get classified right

away. As we get to know them better, we sometimes revise the data we've stored. Pee-Wee Herman quickly gained a niche in many people's minds as a sweet, hyperactive children's TV host. After he was arrested for exposing himself in public (actually, the actor who *portrays* Pee-Wee was arrested) we discovered that his "real" personality didn't match the category we'd created for him, and we added the word scandalous to his description.

It's not just famous people who get this treatment, either. We pigeonhole coworkers as soon as we meet them. You stand at a cocktail party filled with strangers and quickly identify which people are worth a conversation and which might even become friends or lovers. And we do this without a substantial conversation, a background check, or references from trusted friends.

Nancy can't understand why she's having trouble finding a date. Yet whenever she meets someone at a party or through work, the first thing she does is complain. She'll complain about the weather, politics, the economy—it doesn't matter. That's just her nature. Unfortunately for Nancy the pigeonhole she fills is labeled "unhappy complainer."

Compare Nancy to Stan, who always has something nice to say about everyone. He's relentlessly upbeat, and finds the good in every situation. Stan never seems to have trouble finding people to talk with.

Here's a bit of surprising news: At the same time that you're busy pigeonholing everyone you meet, everyone is busy pigeonholing you. They're using trivial information based on your appearance, on your first impression, and on the word of mouth from others to decide where to file you away.

And once you've occupied a pigeonhole, it's incredibly difficult to get out.

## Judging Worksheet

*Here are fifteen pairs of attributes you may encounter in your interactions with other people. Be honest with yourself and figure out which attribute in each pair is likely to endear someone to you and which ones don't matter at all.*

loud.................................................................. thoughtful

bearded ......................................................... clean shaven

clean smelling .................................................. body odor

firm handshake ................................................ wet fish

funny................................................................. serious

speaks well ..................................................... mumbles

famous............................................................. unknown

recommended by a friend ................................. stranger

close talker...................................................... stands back

polite................................................................ boorish

outgoing........................................................... shy

energetic.......................................................... mellow

rich................................................................... poor

lawyer .............................................................. teacher

ex-con.............................................................. policeman

## Your Choice

You have a choice. You can curse the fast-moving, buyer-beware society that created this environment, or you can take control over the judgments made about you. This book is the only book you've ever read about how to do that—understand why people judge you, and learn how to manage the process so it works for you.

If people *really* knew you, really took the time to figure out what you could do for them and how valuable you are, they'd embrace the opportunity to know you, work with you, buy from you, be your friend. If people knew about this good side, you'd have no trouble getting exactly what you deserve out of life. But, unfortunately, very few people are willing to go to those lengths. So it's up to you to take the initiative and determine the output of all the interactions you have today, tomorrow, and forever.

Virtually every day someone makes an erroneous decision about you without enough information. It's no doubt influencing your chances for success in almost everything you try. The good news is that once you recognize that it's going on, you're well on your way to overcoming these prejudices and using them to your advantage.

Getting people to understand how they can benefit from their interaction with you is called marketing. Businesses have been developing this science for decades, studying how to get consumers to buy their products.

That's all marketing is—getting consumers (of any kind) to try or buy products and services. In the next chapter, we'll explain how big companies have used marketing for decades to overcome problems just like yours.

## CHAPTER TWO
# *Marketing*

◆

I̠T TURNS OUT THAT UNDERSTANDING HOW PEOPLE MAKE SNAP decisions and motivating them to make these decisions in your favor has been a problem facing businesses for more than a century. The science of understanding how people create a mental image for a product or service is called marketing. And businesses that know how to market are *always* more successful than those that don't.

Unlike the hit-and-miss personal events of job interviews, speeding tickets, and shopping trips, marketers are able to measure and record which techniques work and which ones don't. They know within days if a new ad is effective or if a direct mail piece is bringing sales. Phone salesmen can tell within minutes if a new script is going to increase their sales or make them plummet.

## Classic Marketing

Coca-Cola used marketing, and nothing but marketing, to take an ordinary sugared beverage and turn it into a multibillion-dollar brand. The product wasn't unique. There were no patents, no special distribution, no price advantage.

Nike used marketing to invent an entire industry—increasing the amount of money spent on "sneakers" by fifty times.

Marlboro cigarettes dominate an industry filled with generic copycats solely because of marketing.

Because marketing results can be measured, and because a company's profit margin is on the line, billions of dollars have been spent trying to improve marketing for businesses. Over the years, an entire discipline has been created. You can get a doctorate in marketing from the Harvard Business School, and there are hundreds of thousands of people who make their money as professional marketers.

Classic marketing grew up with mass production, TV, and the growth of this country. It's all about big ad campaigns, giant promotions, focus groups, and research. Guerrilla marketing is different.

## Guerrilla Marketing

When Jay invented guerrilla marketing about twenty years ago, it was designed for the small business. Since then, the guerrilla marketing books have become the most popular series of marketing books of all time and have been used in virtually every business, large and small.

Newspapers around the country have written glowing reviews of the books. Business magazines have incorporated the phrase "guerrilla" in hundreds of articles. Businesses from Jakarta to Australia to California to New York have flown guerrilla experts in to lecture their staffs.

In addition to the books, there's a nationwide seminar network, an on-line server, magazine columns, consulting services, and more. An industry has sprung up, dedicated to satisfying the need businesses have to learn more about guerrilla marketing. Why? What's so special?

Guerrilla marketing is the science of focusing on the small things. The guerrilla recognizes that marketing takes place whether you work at it or not, but to make it work for you, it must be intentional, consistent, and focused.

The guerrilla focuses on individuals, not markets. She understands that people buy from people, not organizations. She realizes that consistency and persistence are more important than brilliance.

Remember, marketing is the skill of figuring out what people want and then communicating to them that you have it. While some of the terminology may seem new to you, the theme is the one you've been living your entire life.

Guerrilla marketing has built more businesses, sold more products, and created more profits than any other new business technique. It works for big businesses and small businesses, and it can work for you.

Guerrillas cut through the clutter. They understand that people are judging them, and they use insightful marketing techniques to grab a position and hold it.

We've proven these methods again and again, and in this process we've helped tens of thousands of small businesses build profitable marketing programs based on our tested principles. The same principles that can help a waterbed company grow from one store to forty, a cigarette go from number thirty-one to number one, or a beer go from a regional success to a worldwide wonder can make things happen for you.

Throughout this book, we'll be sharing the cornerstones of the guerrilla credo. What's important to note is that guerrilla marketing is custom-made for individuals, perfect for you to use in changing the way people see you.

NOTE

Marketing is **not** sales

*and*

Sales is **not** marketing

A marketer works to invent a product or service someone wants. Then she tries to communicate the benefits of that product to an audience.

A salesman, on the other hand, takes a product created by a marketer and works to overcome the resistance that people have to buying anything.

Guerrilla marketing is not designed to turn you into a salesman. It *is* designed to help you develop a product that's so well conceived, so compelling, and so irresistible you won't need to sell anyone on it.

That's important because the resistance with which people respond to salesmen is overwhelming. If you want to try it out, go downtown and try to give away $1 bills to passersby. You'll be amazed at how skeptical people are. If you view sales with distaste, it's probably because you don't want to work to overcome that resistance. It seems unnatural.

Relax. With guerrilla marketing, you don't have to spend that much time selling. Once you discover how to get your message across without selling, you'll find that people are much more receptive to what you have to say.

Throughout this book, we'll talk about true marketing—how to use the indirect pitch that comes from consistent communication so you can overcome resistance in the long run.

## Marketing Yourself

Marketing sounds all well and good for corporations, products, even nonprofit organizations. But why do *people* need to know about marketing? What do we have to sell, and who are we selling to?

It's easy to understand how packaging a bar of soap helps the manufacturer get a consumer to pick it off the shelf and maybe even purchase it. And it's obvious that while there's no significant difference among vodkas, the bottle and ads make a huge difference. But people are different, aren't they?

After all, while soaps and vodkas may be the same, people are different. We maintain that it doesn't matter how different people are. If you can't get past the "package" that each person carries around, you'll never get close enough to discover the real thing. That's why marketing is critical.

Just as businesses are marketing from the moment they enter the marketplace, all of us are marketing all the time, whether we are conscious of it or not. Every new situation creates an arena in which others are forming opinions about us. In this context, a party, a classroom, or an interview is a new marketplace, where virtually every day someone makes an erroneous decision about you without enough information. It's no doubt influencing your potential for success in almost everything you try.

The only difference between marketing a product and marketing a person is that one is usually done intentionally, with profits in mind, and the other is usually done accidentally, with unpredictable results.

The problem is, most people aren't aware that this is marketing. They don't realize that they can take control over these situations just by being conscious of the messages they are sending. The good news is that once you recognize what's going on, you're well on your way to overcoming these prejudices and using them to your advantage.

In this book, you will learn the various marketing tools guerrilla marketers know, and how to use them with commitment and direction to attack each marketplace you enter with the force of a guerrilla.

Sally is someone who did just that. Sally was a top student at one of the nation's best law schools. She was an expert researcher, and winner of a prestigious award for her work in intellectual property law. Sally decided that after graduation, she wanted a job in a small law firm, doing the sort of intellectual property research she was already good at. Her résumé earned her an interview at most of the top firms in New York.

Wearing her best interview suit, she dutifully made the rounds of her interviews. One by one, she was rejected. Distraught, she searched for some clue about why she was getting these results: Was she not speaking intelligently? Was her résumé not up to snuff?

As she looked around the office she was leaving after yet another failed interview, she suddenly realized: Her problem had nothing to do with her interview techniques or qualifications. They were hardly even looking at them—they were hidden behind her young face. Law firms, until recently bastions of paunchy middle-aged white men, just didn't see themselves hiring someone who looked like Sally, no matter how qualified.

Immediately, it was clear what she needed to do. Sally bought the most serious-looking pair of eyeglasses she could find. These $200 monstrosities were straight out of a Hollywood director's idea of a librarian. And they made her look seven years older. Fitted with flat glass, the glasses didn't affect her vision, but they affected the vision of those who met her. The glasses sent a signal about her seriousness, her qualifications, her desire to find a career.

Two weeks later, Sally had guerrilla-marketed herself into a job at a well-respected law firm. She paid attention to how people were responding to her, figured out why, and took control.

This brings us to the Golden Secret of the guerrilla marketer:

> I can control the messages I send
> and my life will be better for it.

Every action, every word, every element of your appearance and your projected personality is noted, recorded, and judged by everyone you meet.

You have two choices: Leave it to chance and hope that people will understand the message you really want to communicate, or take control over the process and send the message you intend to send.

Let's repeat the message, louder this time. Take a minute to think about what it *really* means:

> I CAN CONTROL THE MESSAGES I SEND
> AND MY LIFE WILL BE BETTER FOR IT.

It's really about the *intentionality* of communication. Figure out what it is you want people to understand about you, and then be sure to transmit it. Once you comprehend the power this gives you, and trust in its effectiveness, you may never be misunderstood again.

## The Intentionality of Communication

To gain authority over what conclusions people come to about you, you must be conscious that they can only evaluate what you show them. The fact that you can learn what people respond to is to your advantage, as soon as you choose to use it.

Think about language. We have elaborate systems that define what words and phrases mean and how to effectively communicate meaning verbally. Then we choose our words according to these definitions.

You wouldn't deliberately use a word that would confuse or offend someone or keep him or her from understanding you just because you really liked that word. Or if you did, it would be with the knowledge that you really didn't care what that person thought.

What we're talking about in this book is much the same. You know what people respond to. You know what their biases, prejudices, and preferences are. So speak their language. Instead of playing the victim to their dispositions, tell them what you want them to hear.

## The Biggest Objection

After working with hundreds of people, we've discovered that most people understand the concepts we've outlined here, and they believe that they work. But one nagging thought often holds them back: *It's not me.*

We want to be ourselves. We want to be accepted for who we "really" are, and we want to live our lives without faking it. The idea of "marketing yourself" turns off a lot of people because it brings to mind used-car salesmen and false television advertising.

So instead of marketing ourselves, most of us rely on what we think is our natural self. We shrug off failure and rejection, rationalizing that if people don't like us, it serves them right!

It's thinking like this that leads to disappointment and rejection. It's thinking like this that leads to undeserved failure and the frustration that comes from not getting everything you deserve.

When two people meet, four people are present at the meeting: you as you really are and you as the other person sees you. It's the same for the other guy.

There are two people inside you:

➤ Your accidental self
              *and*
➤ Your intentional self

Your accidental self is the one you were born with. When you were hungry, you cried. Needed a toy? You grabbed it. By the time you were five, you had learned that in the real world, you couldn't always get what you wanted. You learned that you don't burp at the table, scream at the movies, or kick the teacher.

The entire process of growing up in a civilized society is about managing your accidental self. It means delaying something you'd like to do right now in exchange for getting more later. Bill Clinton might want to slug someone in the nose, but the mature side of him decides to wait and work it out in a more civilized manner.

Have you ever said something that you instantly regretted? Blurted out a comment that you wish you could withdraw? That was your accidental self.

When you wake up in the morning and decide to stay in

bed instead of facing a tough meeting at work, that's your accidental self at work again.

By now, you've realized that your accidental self is what many people call your "true self," but that it's also not very attractive. Your accidental self will get you into trouble almost anywhere, and indulging it isn't really compatible with life in our society.

To make up for this, we create the intentional self. The intentional self describes acts we do on purpose. Wearing a tie to work, for example, or being pleasant to a nasty neighbor. Every day, you perform thousands of intentional actions, all with the same objective: getting what you want from other people. If you lived on a desert island, you'd probably revert to an accidental person. You'd scratch and burp and talk to yourself. You'd do whatever you felt like, when you felt like it. But because you're not marooned, you've already chosen to build up your intentional self.

Your intentional self is just an extension of your accidental self. It doesn't change who you are. You don't stop being you when you change your clothes or refrain from an argument.

But given the compromises your accidental self already makes every day, isn't it sensible to go ahead and maximize the benefits of your intentional self? If you're going to wear a tie anyway, why not wear one that pleases the powers that be? If you're going to build a relationship with a colleague, why not make certain he thinks the best of you?

It's unlikely you'd stand up at a New York Rangers hockey game and take off all your clothes just because it's more comfortable. It's unlikely that you'd walk into your boss's office and tell him off just because you feel like it. It's unlikely that you'd let out a loud belch at a fancy restaurant because the urge strikes.

Every day you make major concessions to the norms of society. You wear a necktie even though it hurts your neck. You sit quietly at a funeral, even if you didn't like the guy who died. You leave a tip, even if the service wasn't so good.

It turns out that if you're like most people, you've already done 95 percent of the job of building your intentional self. You go to work every day, rarely punch people, wear a suit when it's appropriate, listen to traffic cops, and pay your bills on time. But you're holding back. You're wasting an awful lot of effort because you won't go all the way. You need to identify that last 5 percent and discover just how far it can take you.

Are you sabotaging yourself by sending self-defeating messages?

Wendy is vice president of a major television network. She's well paid and occupies a position of power and authority. Yet she has trouble earning the respect of many of her colleagues. Why? Because she's uncomfortable shaking their hands. When someone reaches out to her in greeting, she unenthusiastically submits.

Why does this bother people so much? Because shaking hands is a way of establishing equality, a way of showing that you carry no weapon (physically) and no ill-will (mentally). By holding back, Wendy is sending a message: You're not good enough for me—even if that's not what she means.

The thing is, Wendy probably doesn't even realize she's doing this. Wendy's mind is busy with other things—her schedule, her social life, how shy she is with strangers. It doesn't matter. What does matter is that Wendy is sending a misguided signal, and her ignorance of the Golden Secret is costing her relationships and possibly a valuable promotion.

## I CAN CONTROL THE MESSAGES I SEND
## AND MY LIFE WILL BE BETTER FOR IT.

If Wendy realized that making an effort to get past her discomfort of shaking hands would result in people liking and respecting her, she would likely do it. But chances are she doesn't see the connection. How is that possible? Because more often than not, we react rather than respond. What's the difference?

If you *react* to a medicine, your doctor is concerned and changes the prescription.

If you *respond* to a medicine, that's good news. Your body is doing the right thing.

That's sort of the way it works with other people. If you react to them, then you're indulging your emotions, saying and doing what you *want* to do instead of what you *should* do. Reacting makes you happy in the short run. It's your accidental self at work. It's honking your horn, or yelling at your boss, or hiding from a difficult situation. When someone tries to shake her hand, Wendy is reacting to the discomfort she feels in meeting people rather than responding to the person who's offering his hand.

Response is much more measured. It's more mature. It's more successful. A response considers all the factors, especially what's best for your long-term guerrilla marketing campaign. It's considering your intentional self before you indulge your accidental self. A response builds your position, supports who you are, helps you get to where you want to be.

When Walter Mondale criticized Ronald Reagan's age during the Presidential debates, Reagan could have reacted by becoming defensive or ignoring his ill-mannered challenger. Instead, he *responded* by taking the initiative and saying, "I won't make age a factor in this race. My opponent's inexperience won't be brought up by me. . . ."

Think of the many times you've reacted to something someone said or did and then sent messages that ended up hurting you. How could you have altered these to make yourself more successful?

In this book, we're not proposing that you make any compromises you can't live with. We don't want you to adopt any marketing tactics that conflict with the person you'd like to become. We're not encouraging you to lie or be phony. But in our research we've found that knowing the choices and their implications is far better than not knowing. This book is about managing your intentional self, about learning how to define and manage the message you send.

And here's the coolest part of all—once you've done something long enough, it stops being part of your conscious intentional self and becomes an ingrained habit. In short: If you do it long enough, it becomes you.

Smile a lot, be nice to people, and soon you'll become a nice person. Act like you respect your job while you're at work, and soon you'll come to respect it while you're at home. Raise your hand in class, and soon you'll discover you have more to say.

These are powerful concepts. They've been demonstrated again and again. Adopt them and make them a conscious part of your life and they will become a natural part of your life. In a nutshell: Act like the person you'd like to be, because that's the person you'll become.

## Who Are Your Customers?

Okay, so you're a marketer. Now what?

The most important person in a guerrilla marketer's life is the customer. Without a customer, there is no marketing.

If you don't know who your customer is, though, you don't have a chance of creating a marketing program that works. A Presidential candidate spends millions on polling—just to find out what his "customers" think. IBM cares very deeply about the buying habits of the five hundred top computer managers at the five hundred biggest companies across the country. Ralph at the corner deli doesn't carry zabaglione because his customers don't want it.

Just as these businesses large and small are well aware of their customers, you're going to need to get a better handle on yours. Your boss, your friends, your spouse—they're all customers.

You're probably saying, "Wait a second—I don't *market* myself to my friends! And especially not to my spouse." But that's not true. Every time you're in a situation where someone else is interpreting your messages, you're marketing yourself. You're sending messages to your spouse all the time, whether they are ones of appreciation, indifference, resentment, or love. The fact that so many of us are unaware of sending these messages doesn't mean we're not marketing ourselves—it just means we're not marketing ourselves accurately.

When your best friend describes you, what does he or she say? If you could choose a description, do you think it would be different from the one your boss would give? What about the people you knew in high school? What about your spouse?

Did you answer each of these questions differently? Most likely you did. Because you probably act differently with your boss than you do with your spouse, and your friendships now are probably different than they were in high school.

No news there. We all know that who we're dealing with

dictates how we act. We're going to show you how to do this intentionally, to use your marketing skills to go after your goals instead of just having things happen to you.

Here are the people most of us market ourselves to without even thinking about it:

➤ **Teachers.** From the first day you showed up in kindergarten, you've been marketing yourself to teachers. What role did you play in the classroom? Did you sit up front, bright-eyed and bushy-tailed, or in the last row, slouched and doodling? What kind of responses did you get from your teachers? Were they the kind you would have liked to have gotten? If not, what could you have done to change it?

➤ **Parents and Children.** These people are such an immediate part of our lives that most of us don't give them the same kind of thought that we do to our other relationships. Yet marketing is an integral aspect of family interactions. Kids learn from an early age what their parents respond to. If they cry, kick, and scream, do they get the cookie they've been after, or does it take a coy grin and a "pretty please?" And how parents respond to their children affects the image the kids develop of them; acting distant or distracted doesn't communicate warmth or affection, even if that's what a parent truly feels. How do you relate to your parents even now?

➤ **Bosses.** Your boss may not spend much time examining the actual content of your work or the actual results of your efforts. She is, however, aware of your image, your attitude, the word of mouth of your coworkers and customers, and your relationship with her. The biggest reason employees don't get promoted is that they don't market themselves up. A cynic will call it kissing up to the boss, but the cynic is wrong. The way you transmit your skills, talents, desires, and interests to the boss directly translates into your position and influences your income. There's a difference between empty flattery and a deliberate, focused attempt to let the people you work for understand what you stand for, what you're good at, and what you contribute. What kind of interactions do you have with your boss? Are they getting you where you'd like to be?

➤ **Prospective Employers.** Finding a job is little more than marketing once you have the skills you need for the post. Few companies will take the time to give you a week-long trial period. Instead, they look at your marketing, your positioning, your reputation, your appearance, your attitude, and your background. Market yourself well in this category and you won't look long before you find a job.

➤ **Employees.** If you manage someone, they're judging you. Your employees are always working to categorize you, to understand you, to second-guess what you're trying to say. Why is it that some bosses are able to get so much more out of their employees? It's because they communicate their position to them in many different ways. What do you convey with your management style?

➤ **Buyers.** Whenever you sell *anything*, people are judging you. They judge your brochure, your phone voice, your appearance, and reputation. A major study found that more than 80 percent of all major purchase decisions by large corporate buyers are made within *thirty seconds* of meeting a salesperson. Not because of price or service or guarantee. These decisions are based solely on the personal marketing of the salesperson. Notice we said thirty seconds not thirty minutes. It is all about split-second decisions. How does your sales pitch come off? Do you immediately win the confidence of your buyer?

➤ **Mates.** Does it surprise you that we're talking about

marketing yourself to your spouse? Who better to market to than the person you're going to spend your entire life with? If you wear nice clothes instead of rags for a night out, you're marketing. You're telling her that you don't take her for granted, that she's important and worth dressing up for.

There's nothing insincere or manipulative about marketing yourself to your spouse. Quite the opposite. The husband who doesn't care what his wife thinks, who doesn't take the time to present his true self in the best possible light, is showing contempt for his wife.

➤ **Prospective Mates.** They don't call it a blind date for nothing. In the first few seconds, then the first few hours, then the first few weeks of dating, we're busy making decisions. It's hard to believe, but you probably made the decision to get seriously involved with your mate within hours or days of meeting him. If you tend to get shy and quiet, make the effort to market yourself with a friendly smile and warm introduction, and you're far more likely to find someone willing to dig deep, to uncover your real wishes, feelings, desires, and hopes. Ignore the power of marketing and you'll probably never even get a chance.

➤ **Friends.** Most of us hang out with people like us. But how do we tell if someone's like us? How do we separate that one best friend from the dozens at the first college mixer? How do we decide who to have dinner with and who to send just an annual Christmas note to? People are always assessing how compatible you are with how they see themselves, and you're doing the same with them. Take a hard look at the people who are your closest friends. Then look at your family's friends. You'll start to see patterns. If you're like most people, your friends share a similar set of attributes and attitudes.

➤ **Coworkers.** You spend more of your waking hours with coworkers than with anyone else, even your spouse. Yet few of us take the time to build the image we want at work, to gain the reputation we'd really like to have. Determining how you want to be perceived and working to deliver on that is a critical factor in enjoying the time you spend at work. How do you present yourself in the workplace? How do people respond to you?

➤ **Sellers.** Salesmen aren't the only people who sell. Every time you meet a salesperson, the way you market yourself will help determine the quality of the service you get. If you communicate through your personal marketing that you're not going to accept anything less than excellent, truthful salesmanship, you're far more likely to get it. Think of people you've seen in car showrooms or buying computer equipment. One potential customer is carrying a clipboard and several copies of reviews and articles. The other is standing there with a harried husband and a screaming child. Which person is going to get better service? Who's going to pay more in exchange for a quick sale?

➤ **Landlords.** Why do some people always seem to have trouble with their landlords and superintendents, and others never do? Is it possible that the interactions, the personal marketing, the signals sent back and forth set the tone for the relationship? Do you take the time to be courteous to your landlord, recognizing that having this person see you as trustworthy and responsible could make your life easier in the future, or did you make the decision that it's just not worth the effort for the number of times you'll have to deal with this person? What kind of relationship do you have with your landlord; have you made the right choice?

➤ **Clients and Customers.** Stew Leonard, the legendary

supermarket king, has a two-thousand-pound granite block sitting outside his flagship store. Engraved in the block is

Rule One: The Customer Is Always Right
Rule Two: If the Customer Is Wrong, See Rule One

Do you think this obvious display of personal marketing helps the relationship between Stew and his customers? Every interaction between you and a customer determines the way the customer thinks of you and has a direct bearing on your income.

➤ **Neighbors.** Why do some people manage to have wonderful relationships with their neighbors, almost like Rhoda and Mary, while others can't manage one pleasant interchange? Do you see being amiable to your neighbors as a chore impinging on your time at home or a way to make that time better? Every time you decide either to go over and say hello or not to bother is a step toward building lifelong friendships or long-term animosity.

➤ **Professionals.** Ever been to a doctor who treated you like a statistic? Or hoped for a solid relationship with a lawyer, only to find yourself talked down to? Does Colin Powell get treated like that by his doctor? How about Donald Trump and his lawyer? You don't have to be rich or famous to be treated well by a highly paid professional. But you do need to identify the marketing techniques that will gain you respect and proper treatment.

➤ **Your Community.** What do the people in town think of you? Are you known as a philanthropist or a misanthrope? Do people respect you and your family? Do you feel a part of the community, or would you rather be left alone? Think about what you want from a community, then think about whether your current actions and attitudes toward people will get you there. There are simple steps you can take to create a marketing program that will build your status in the community, no matter how large or small.

➤ **Family.** Are you the black sheep? Does Aunt Myra point out how sad she is that you're not married? Is your father-in-law still sorry you married his daughter? How much more would you enjoy the holidays if your family understood who you are and respected you for it? Instead of just sitting back and resenting them, you could take the first step toward changing the relationship.

➤ **The Police.** Have you ever been stopped by a cop? How do they decide who to suspect of shoplifting and who to give a break to on a minor traffic violation? If your house were burglarized and you needed their help, how can you market yourself to get quick, professional help from them? How does your manner change when you get pulled over for speeding?

Bankers, clergy, strangers, and more—there are dozens of constituencies left, groups that make determinations about you whenever they see you. If you're leaving marketing to these people to chance, you probably won't be happy with the results. These are the people who control whether or not you get what you deserve. Marketing to them is the critical step in realizing your dreams.

# CHAPTER THREE

# Five Things Every Marketer Knows

◆

IN THIS CHAPTER, WE'RE GOING TO OUTLINE THE SECRETS OF product marketing. We'll show you exactly which concepts are critical to success, and why. Once you understand how a product or service can make an impression on you, you'll be in a position to figure out how you make an impression with your most important commodity: yourself.

There are five concepts you need to understand. Here's a mini-MBA course in marketing:

1. **Clutter.** The condition of the marketplace that makes marketing necessary—too many products in too little space.
2. **Pigeonholes.** The simplified categories that result from using shortcuts to cut through the clutter.
3. **Positioning.** How marketers identify themselves in the face of shortcuts and pigeonholing.
4. **Features and Benefits.** Complimentary factors that go into a product or person's positioning.
5. **Goals.** The driving force behind any marketing campaign.

## Clutter

Last year, if you're anything like the average American, you saw more than one million commercials and advertisements. You met several hundred (perhaps thousand) new people, were exposed to countless ideas, concepts, and changes, and probably encountered more than ten thousand people you had never seen before and will likely never see again. The sensation is like a movie being played before your eyes, but it's running at a very, very high speed.

In marketing terms, this is called clutter. Clutter refers to the crowding and confusion in the marketplace caused by the unbelievable number of products and services people are trying to sell.

The amount of clutter out there is astonishing. There are too many products chasing too few dollars. Advertisers can choose from five television networks, fifty cable channels, thirteen million web pages, three thousand magazines, and another three thousand newspapers.

The average supermarket carries about thirty thousand items. Yet last year, an astonishing seventeen thousand new products were introduced. Last night, you probably watched an hour or two of television. Eager marketers spent millions of dollars sponsoring those shows, and there were probably sixty commercials shown while you were watching. Can you list them? Can you remember even a dozen? How about five?

As a consumer, you've been bombarded with advertising your entire life. At times, it seems as though every marketer on earth is trying to get you to buy something—today.

We take shortcuts. We make decisions according to subconscious associations we have developed through time and experience. It doesn't take much to build an association, but it takes a lot to knock it down. The challenge of the corporate marketer is to grab your attention, avoid stereotypes, and get the message across. Your challenge in marketing yourself to other people is exactly the same.


## Pigeonholes

In the face of the huge amount of information that's hurled at us every day, it's a wonder we just don't give up and stick our heads in the ground.

In many cases, that's exactly what people do. In the face of information overload, we force everything into a pigeonhole. Whether we like it or not, everything is stereotyped and filed. People, products, places . . . it doesn't matter. There's not enough time and not enough space to get the full story.

We pigeonhole products according to their reputation and their advertising. We don't give the process much thought, if any, but it happens. Our minds are conditioned to look for cues.

It works much the same with people. In order to keep track of everything we learn, we subconsciously put people into categories. We all do it. By now, it's an automatic response. Everyone we meet gets unconsciously defined right away. We pigeonhole celebrities and coworkers alike. The fact that this actually takes place is clear when you think of how we stand at cocktail parties filled with strangers and quickly identify which people are worth talking to and who we'd like to know better. Even longtime acquaintances get categorized according to our understanding of them.

And once you've occupied a pigeonhole, it's incredibly difficult to get out. So you might as well pick your own pigeonhole. You're going to be there a long time. Find a good one!

## Positioning

A good marketer knows that, like it or not, she and her products are going to get pigeonholed. Positioning is nothing more than pigeonholing yourself on purpose.

The theory is pretty simple: There are too many products on the market, and most people will just ignore most of them. If you're lucky enough to make an impact with your product marketing, you want to find one position that you can stake out in the customer's brain, one attribute or benefit, or whatever, that you communicate and defend.

Mercedes doesn't make cheap cars. Their position is that they make heavy, expensive, responsive, safe cars for middle-aged executives. Of course, Mercedes cars are a lot of things. They're very fast, for example. They hold their resale value. They last a long time. They come with a first aid kit in the trunk. They're roomy. But the folks at Mercedes don't mention any of that in their positioning and advertising. Instead, they focus on the core values they want you to remember about their cars. They realize that if they tell you too much, you'll remember nothing.

Yugo *did* make cheap cars. And that was their position. They didn't talk about reliability, resale value, or anything else. They just reminded people how cheap they were. Unfortunately for Yugo, being cheap just wasn't enough. It never is. Of all the product sold in all the stores in the United States, none of the leaders are the cheapest brands.

Ben & Jerry's doesn't talk about how many chunks are in every container of their ice cream. They don't focus on where the strawberries are grown or how many calories are inside. Instead, they positioned themselves as a brand made by real people, with real ideals.

Nike started out positioning itself as a maker of shoes for athletes. They let Keds and Converse and Puma and Adidas make just plain sneakers. Nike made shoes for real runners.

Marlboro cigarettes used to be positioned as a cigarette for women. They had a fancy box and feminine marketing. Then Leo Burnett advertising invented Marlboro Country, with cowboys and ranches and macho music. Since then, the position of the cigarette hasn't changed in thirty years. Marlboro doesn't have to talk about convenience or value or make a lot of jokes. They've positioned themselves as the American cigarette, the cigarette of freedom, cowboys, and rugged individualists.

Crest is a toothpaste that fights cavities. UltraBrite is a toothpaste that gives you sex appeal. Tom's of Maine is all natural. Three very different positions. Of course, all three toothpastes do essentially the same thing, but your impression of them is very different.

Think there's a big difference in vodka? By law, they're all made the same way. Yet Absolut has a very different position than Stolichnaya, and most drinkers of one brand hesitate to switch to the other.

*Many marketers resist positioning. They'd like to believe that their product is so compelling, so interesting, so unique that consumers will want to hear about* all *the product attributes,* all *the marvelous reasons to use it. The result is that they hear none of them. By refusing to allow themselves to be pigeonholed, these marketers end up being ignored.*

Seven-Up was a fourth-rate product success. It had average distribution, small market share, and not much recognition among the public. Then the marketers came up with a great positioning statement. They called it the Uncola. What they meant was that whatever you thought about Coke or Pepsi, Seven-Up was the opposite. If they were too sweet, Seven-Up was refreshing. If they were dark, Seven-Up was clear. If they were the official beverage of the gang, Seven-Up stood for being independent.

It worked. Seven-Up saw its sales skyrocket. Its message stood out, especially in the counterculture sixties and seventies, where being part of the crowd wasn't necessarily such a good thing.

Seven-Up was all these things—clear, refreshing, different, before it was the Uncola. But the title could promise all of that, and the product came through.

Here are five products. See if you can figure out the position of each:

1. Boston Chicken
2. Apple Macintosh
3. Prudential
4. Sprint
5. Saturn

You may have always been confident, hardworking, motivated, and eager. But until you make the conscious decision to position yourself that way, and promise those things to the people you work for, they aren't going to get you the results you want.

A key part of this book is learning how to position yourself. The people you meet just aren't going to take the time to get to know you. They're going to make a snap decision about who you are and what you stand for whether you want them to or not.

*Most of us don't like to accept this.* Just like the marketers who resist positioning their products, most of us don't want to boil down the essence of our personality to just eight words. Most of us don't have a plan and solid goals. And most of us fail more than we ought to.

Madonna is one of the most famous women in the world. But we have no idea what books she likes, whether she knows how to bake cookies, and if she remembers her friends' birthdays. Madonna has positioned herself as an individualist, as strong-willed, sexy, independent, and talented, and we've pigeonholed her according to the guidelines she's set.

Abraham Lincoln has a position in our minds. Honest guy with beard who freed the slaves. Eight words. Compare this with Grover Cleveland, Millard Fillmore, U. S. Grant, and even James R. Polk. These Presidents all worked just as hard as Lincoln, but because they have no position, we don't have a good idea of who they are or what they stood for.

Not convinced? Think positioning only works for products and famous people? Go back to your high school days. Who do you remember? Why? Chances are the people who stand out in your memory aren't necessarily the ones you spent the most time with, but they are the ones with the most vivid positioning.

And then there were those people who you didn't pay any attention to, until you got the locker next to theirs or sat next to them in class, only to discover that they were really nice or interesting. They probably didn't position themselves at all.

We know ourselves very, very well. We're aware of all our skills, our talents, our pluses, and our minuses. And quite often, we expect that others will know this, too. We meet someone at a cocktail party and are surprised and offended when they walk off after just a couple of minutes. "Wait! I'm so interesting! How can you leave?"

Sam knew from the moment he met Rachel that they were right for each other. And as they got to know each other he was more and more convinced. They had everything in common, they were both easygoing and liked to have a good time, and Sam knew that if he got the chance he could build a great life with her.

But Rachel never showed any interest. She dated the football quarterback, the flamboyant rich kid, the biker. Each with his own vibrant position. But not Sam.

Sam didn't despair. And he didn't change his positioning, either. He didn't start working out or buy a Corvette or die his hair pink. Instead, he worked hard to reinforce his position as the honest guy, the industrious guy, the guy who was nice to everyone he met.

A few months later, Rachel got tired of boy shopping. She began to look for someone who stood for things that mattered. A few months later, she started dating Sam. Seven years and two kids later, they're as happy as ever.

Sam knew what he had to offer Rachel. And he hoped and hoped that she would somehow know, too. But unfortunately, most people aren't usually as interested in you as you are. There are a lot of people out there to meet and get to know. If you want people to remember or be intrigued by you, you need to show them why. You need a position.

### Once More on Positioning
Here are three painkillers:

➤ Advil
➤ Alleve
➤ Anacin

Why should you take any of these instead of Tylenol? We have no idea, and you probably don't either. These are probably very fine pain relievers, but the marketers behind them haven't taken the time to explain why you should switch. The result, of course, is that you probably won't.

Here are some other brands that don't position themselves very well, and as a result, suffer from a lack of growth:

➤ Burger King
➤ National Rent a Car
➤ Adidas
➤ RC Cola

These brands, on the other hand, do a great job of positioning themselves:

➤ NBC Must See TV
➤ McDonald's
➤ Donald Trump

Several "brands" got positioned despite their best efforts:

➤ Politicos like Richard Bork and Richard Nixon
➤ Movies like *Heaven's Gate* and *Waterworld*

Nixon didn't set out to be remembered as a crook. Bork isn't happy that the Democrats positioned him as an extremist.

You probably have never seen *Heaven's Gate* or *Waterworld*. That's the point—even though you have no personal information on whether these movies were any good, the media, and thus the public, remembers them as all-time examples of Hollywood greed gone awry.

The effect of purposeful marketing on success in these examples is clear. Can you place your personal image on this scale of positioning?

## Positioning Quiz

Here are three positioning categories, with four products or people in each category. See how quickly you can identify the position of each brand.

BEER
    Samuel Adams
    Budweiser
    Heineken
    Red Dog

MOVIE ACTORS/ACTRESSES
    Jack Nicholson
    Meg Ryan
    Clint Eastwood
    Rosie Perez

TV CHARACTERS
    Doug Ross
    George Costanza
    June Cleaver
    The Fonz

## Answers

BEER
    Samuel Adams—the best beer made in America
    Budweiser—the party beer that everyone likes
    Heineken—a yuppie beer

Red Dog—the cheap but smooth beer for people who want to get drunk

## MOVIE ACTORS/ACTRESSES
Jack Nicholson—intense, slightly crazy guy
Meg Ryan—sweet, smiley romantic interest
Clint Eastwood—cowboy and reticent, all-around tough guy
Rosie Perez—fast-talking, bouncy Latin American

## TV CHARACTERS
Doug Ross—thirty-something, competent pediatrician, womanizer with a fear of commitment
George Costanza—a loser
June Cleaver—caring, efficient, normal mother and housewife
The Fonz—motorcycle riding, popular, sensitive tough guy

How quickly did you respond to these products and names? Was it obvious what the position of each one was? Did you come to the same conclusions we did?

Which beer do you like better: St. Pauli Girl or Beck's Light? St. Pauli Girl is marketed as a good-time beer for college kids (right down to the scantily clad woman on the label) while Beck's is for power-crazed yuppies. Yet both bottles are brewed at the same brewery, and it is impossible to tell them apart in a blind taste test. It's the positioning that matters here, not the beer.

Positioning is hard. No brand, no matter how big or how popular, and no person, no matter how interesting and intelligent, can be all things to all people. Marketers have to be extra careful about the tendency to broaden a message; while it may seem that you'll reach more people by doing so, by diffusing your focus you effectively reach none.

The same is true for you. There are always going to be

people who like you and people who don't, people you're meant to get to know and people with whom you'll get no further than the first impression. But that's okay.

If you position yourself vividly, the people who are likely to want to be with you will be able to recognize that fast and easily and not pass up the chance because of mixed or missed messages. Will you lose opportunities by not being Mr. Bland? Of course. But in the long run, not offending anyone is worse than offending no one.

Someone who needs darts can easily pinpoint the store in Manhattan that sells darts. Because that's *all* they sell. They don't sell scuba equipment, billiard tables, or roller blades. They sell darts. You can guess two things about this company: First, they're not as big as Herman's or any other giant chain. Second, they're doing just fine, thanks. People who are really into darts know that this is the store for them.

If you position yourself as outgoing, fun-loving, and up-beat, someone who likes to have a good time will readily single you out as a person they'd like to spend time with, in the same way that someone who needs a lightbulb would go straight to Just Bulbs, a store that specializes in—you guessed it—all kinds of bulbs. Want a shade to go with that? You won't find it at Just Bulbs, but you will find it at Just Shades, a little ways uptown.

Will someone come along who is put off by your always sunny disposition? No question about it. So what?

Of course, product or business positioning doesn't mean you have to be a specialist in what you offer. A brand can be positioned by:

➢ price
➢ service

➢ selection
➢ location
➢ size
➢ quality
➢ guarantee
➢ and a dozen other variables

And people aren't only positioned by personality. Other factors are also important:

➢ attitude
➢ appearance
➢ body language
➢ speech
➢ profession
➢ references
➢ innumerable other intangibles

Painless dentists, honest auto mechanics, and class clowns have all discovered that people will respond to someone who stands out from the crowd.

Of course, no one can force you to market yourself. You can reject the entire system and insist on "being yourself." That's your privilege. But even if you don't consciously choose a position, you still have one. It may be muddy, inconsistent, and difficult to detect, but just about everyone you meet is going to pick one for you anyway. You may think, *I don't want to do any marketing for myself.* But that just means that the marketing you are doing, consciously or unconsciously, probably won't help you achieve your goals.

This is one of the key messages of the art of Guerrilla Marketing Yourself. *You must choose a position or have it chosen for you.*

Guerrillas learn early on that they must select their own position, that they must consistently use it, and they have to stick with it. The position you choose for yourself will determine who you become friends with, where you work, and how high you get promoted. Of course your position can evolve. It can grow and change with you.

You can't just pick a position out of thin air, of course. You can't decide to go from being a shy bartender with a passion for roses to becoming a glamorous Wall Street analyst with a harem of attractive men standing at your beck and call. Just as Seven-Up started from a base (the soft drink business) you must stick with your essence.

The message behind positioning yourself isn't to invent something brand-new out of whole cloth. In fact, it's exactly the opposite. You position yourself well when you capture part of your essence in a few simple symbols and phrases. *You must choose a position you can live with, a position you can be proud of, a position you can deliver.*

All too often, people unconsciously position themselves in very unattractive ways. These are good people, talented people, but people who are sabotaging their lives by focusing on an element of their personality that others dislike.

A meeting with Suzie is always a tense affair. As long as things are going well, Suzie is smiling, going about her business. But as soon as she senses that she's about to get "in trouble," Suzie tightens up. She points her finger somewhere else, or pouts.

This *reaction* to stressful situations, combined with her youthful dress and overall appearance, does not lead to a positive overall impression. She's immature, prone to temper tantrums and blaming sessions. Suzie doesn't rein in her feelings—when she feels like saying something, she does.

Suzie signs her name with a lowercase *s*. In short, she looks and acts as if she's sixteen years old.

Suzie is a book editor at a prestigious New York publishing house. How far do you suppose she's going to go in publishing? Is she going to attract the authors she needs to build a career? Is her boss going to go out of his way to give her the very best projects? Not likely.

Suzie's chosen a position for herself. It's unlikely that she did it consciously, but it's already damaging her career and her professional relationships.

Can Suzie find a different position and still be true to her nature? Of course she can. Suzie is a good writer, and she has a knack for finding good books in a pile of slush. Suzie could compensate for her youthfulness by working extra hard to act and look more mature. She could call herself Susan. She could listen and speak in measured tones. She could avoid throwing temper tantrums and work at emulating her more experienced colleagues. She could trade in her contact lenses for more serious glasses and change her hairstyle. In short, by stressing her positives, Suzie could turn everything around.

Jackie, on the other hand, is in a good position. She came to the United States from England. When she first arrived here, people who heard her speak immediately recognized the accent and identified her as British. But Jackie wanted to fit in, so she tried her best to speak without it. Later, when she entered the pet supply business, she soon learned that when she allowed herself to use the accent, she was able to sell far more than when she tried to sound like a Yankee. Turns out that people in the United States associate a London accent with sophistication. So Jackie stopped trying to be who she wasn't and her business is booming. Can her British accent be given some of the credit? Ask Jackie. She thinks so.

## Some Sample Positions

Here are some short descriptions of positioning statements we've seen for people just like you. Most of these are pretty clearly drawn—not a lot of ambivalence here. See if you recognize someone you know:

> ➤ a smart, caring teacher
> ➤ a fixer, eager to make everything okay
> ➤ an impatient, mean screamer
> ➤ a selfish, self-centered person who's always right
> ➤ an oddball inconoclast, eager to do anything that doesn't fit in
> ➤ a back-of-the-bus, spitball-throwing troublemaker
> ➤ a kind, patient, sympathetic listener
> ➤ a slow-moving but smart lug
> ➤ an insincere friend of the moment
> ➤ a painfully shy recluse
> ➤ employee of the year
> ➤ an insecure neurotic, always laughing and smiling to hide the pain
> ➤ a wise guru, always ready with insightful advice or a shoulder to cry on
> ➤ a thoughtful, reliable friend
> ➤ an underqualified hack, in over his head
> ➤ a power-hungry, macho cop

You get the idea. Of course, no one is like this all the time. But given just a few minutes to make a decision, most of us have categorized people into one or more of these slots.

## The Cost of Positioning

*You can't be everything to everyone.* When you stake out a position, you lose some customers. When you stake out a position, you can't mention every good thing about your product. When you stake out a position, you make it easier for the other guy to take potshots at you. But it's worth it. A position makes you stand out. Remember: *You remain anonymous unless you position yourself.*

Stop for a second and think about the people you saw at the supermarket yesterday. The ones you remember are almost certainly the ones who stood out for some reason. Now list three of your coworkers. Did you list the ones that blend into the woodwork or the ones that stand out?

## The Rule of Positioning

*If you can't describe your position in eight words or less, you don't have a position.*

Marketers frequently fall in love with their products, and they assume everyone else does, too. They expect busy consumers to spend hours of time poring over brochures, reviews, and special reports. They're certain that word of mouth and referrals will build their brand to great heights, but they ignore the certain truth of the cluttered world of the nineties: People don't care that much.

People, of course, do the same thing. We're frustrated that we don't get what we deserve, because we *know* that if the other person would just take the time, they'd realize how great we are.

You get only one chance to make a first impression. One chance to stake out a niche, a position in the mind of the prospect. Sometimes a new product comes along and does a great job of that. Miller Lite, for example, will always be remembered as a great-tasting beer that doesn't fill you up.

Nice work! But usually, we ignore the millions of dollars of advertising that marketers throw at us every day.

Hence, our positioning rule: *If you can't describe your position in eight words or less, you don't have a position.* You must keep a position succinct and focused in order for it to stand out from the innumerable messages we are all receiving all the time. By keeping your personal statement short and sweet, you have a better chance of getting your message across—and making it stick.

Do you make a first impression? Have you thought about it, worked on it, tested it, refined it? What about your second, third, and fourth impressions?

—————————— **So What's Your Position?** ——————————

*Here's an essential guerrilla exercise. Ask four friends and/or coworkers to fill out the following form. Encourage (beg!) them to be honest with you. Without understanding your current, unconscious position, you'll never be able to craft a new, more effective position.*

*REMEMBER! You can't invent a new position out of thin air. We've already talked about the difficulty you'll have if the position you choose doesn't match the person that you are deep down. Our goal isn't to invent a new person—it's to best express the person you are right now.*

*This is a two-step exercise. In the first step, your friends identify where on each measure you rate compared to other people they know. In the second step, they are to circle the six things that stand out the most about you from these thermometers. These six attributes aren't the only things you project. But they are the things that are most outstanding, the things that get you pigeonholed.*

attractive............................................................ unattractive

brilliant .......................................................................... dim

calculating ............................................................ emotional

caring................................................................................ cold

classy ......................................................................... brassy

competent............................................................ incompetent

cultured............................................................................ coarse

driven........................................................................... passive

easygoing .................................................................... fussy

| | |
|---|---|
| enthusiastic | bored |
| ethical | immoral |
| experienced | novice |
| fascinating | boring |
| fast | slow |
| helping | needy |
| giving | selfish |
| honest | dishonest |
| intellectual | down-to-earth |
| kind | cruel |
| mature | immature |
| outgoing | shy |
| patient | impatient |
| rational | emotional |
| secure | insecure |
| smart | unintelligent |
| smiling | sour |
| sultry | cold |
| superficial | deep |
| tardy | prompt |

*Have you found your current positioning statement? Are you happy with it? If so, sit down and write it out right now. If not, hold on while we give you some more tactics to help you construct a new one.*

## Features and Benefits

Guerrilla marketers know that every product or service has features. Automatic door locks. Insulated windows. A fur collar. Overnight delivery. They also know that no one buys features. They buy benefits. *No one ever bought a drill bit. Millions of people have bought a hole.* That may seem cryptic, but read it again. It's worth it.

Turning a feature into a benefit is simple—figure out what the feature does for someone, and describe it. Probably no one has ever really craved a bright, shiny, new drill bit. But they have really needed to be able to screw their new bed together, and they need that drill to do it.

One of the challenges of marketing is finding the benefits that people want.

Here's another way to think about it: Marketers make promises, then keep them. They make a promise when they tell you that a product quenches thirst or reminds you of the Old West or removes warts or makes you look good. And they keep promises when the product they helped create actually does what they said it was going to do.

Federal Express made a brilliant promise, "When it absolutely, positively has to be there overnight." Then they kept it. That simple marketing equation is responsible for billions in profits and the birth of an entire industry.

People define benefits from their own point of view. *They don't care if a feature helps someone else.* When they consider a product, they're looking for something that will improve their lives—the sooner the better. Some people see a cordless phone as offering them the chance to walk around the house while they use it. Others like being able to keep it by the TV while waiting for it to ring. Same features, different benefits.

The same is true for personal marketing. Of course people are impressed when you say you went to Harvard. But your boss will forget that initial respect pretty fast if you don't do your job well. Harvard is a feature. The benefit is that your smarts will help them grow their business. Few care if you can bench-press 180 pounds—but some people care a lot about how that makes you look, or how you can help them move those boxes.

Don't be in such a hurry to sell every feature you've got on your résumé. Instead, figure out what your prospective boss, spouse, or friend *wants,* then stress that.

As you look down your list of skills and attributes, think about it from the point of view of the people you'll be meeting—what have you got to offer them? Then try to construct a position that's based on benefits, not features.

──────── **Features and Benefits Worksheet** ────────

## JAY'S FEATURES AND BENEFITS

*Feature*                         *Benefit*

fast typist................................speed of completing assignments

always meets deadlines ........certainty of keeping promises

not a prima donna .................easy to work with

enthusiastic ...........................writes excitingly

quick learner .........................able to tackle complex assignments

hard worker............................handles even very complicated tasks

many interests........................can generate enthusiasm for anything

fascinated with technology ....unafraid of new advancements

optimistic ...............................rarely in a bad or down mood

flexible ...................................able to live with changes

## WHAT ARE YOURS?

*Feature*                         *Benefit*

_____       _____

_____       _____

_____       _____

_____       _____

_____       _____

_____       _____

_____       _____

_____

## Goals

Why do some people always manage to get what they want? Is it nothing but hard work and focus? There are two reasons that most people overlook:

> ➤ They know what they want.
> ➤ They communicate it.

Much of this book is about the second—and most difficult—element. But all the communication skills in the world won't help you if you don't know what you want.

Shooting arrows with a blindfold on is almost as silly as living life without goals. No guerrilla marketer unveils an expensive, time-consuming marketing plan without first determining her goals, and you shouldn't either.

A guerrilla marketer can tell you exactly who she's selling to. She can describe in detail the benefits the prospect wants. And, she can describe the best possible outcome—her goal.

What, exactly, are you after? Do you want a date, a job, a sale, a promotion? Do you want more friends, a more peaceful marriage, success at work, time to yourself? If you're like most people, you've lived your life sort of randomly, never writing down exactly what it is you want.

*Maybe where you are right now is exactly where you deserve to be.* "No," you say, "I was qualified for that promotion." Or "I'm way more fun to be with than the people who got invited to that party." But by intentionally not making the decision to communicate these things about yourself, you missed out. Maybe you *are* more fun, but if you seem unapproachable or uninterested, nobody will invite you. And no matter how qualified you are, if you don't communicate your professionalism through your personal presentation in the office you'll probably stay where you are.

Whether or not you choose to control these things is up to you. If being able to wear whatever you want whenever you want to is something you don't want to change, that's fine. But this book is about realizing that by making this choice, you're making a trade-off.

Set your priorities. Know what you want. If your chief goal is a casual life and one of your priorities is working in an environment that will accept your choice, then your jeans and tee-shirt are great. But be aware that those jeans will not help you if you are aiming for a job as an executive in a high-profile firm. Each step you take should be a conscious movement toward what you want.

Remember, *every* goal involves an exchange. You can't have everything—there isn't enough time and money in the world for that to happen. If you want to get in shape, you can't eat an ice cream sundae for lunch every day. If you want to spend more time at home, you probably can't spend more time at work as well.

In addition to the trade-offs that come from prioritizing your goals, you need to identify whether your objectives are realistic given your resources. An entrepreneur met with Seth some years ago, and explained how his new technology was going to enable him to build a billion-dollar business. Here is the marketing strategy he had in mind: Buy one thirty-second commercial on *The Cosby Show*, even though it would take his entire advertising budget, because that would get him the attention he needed for his business to succeed.

Kudos to him for setting a goal, but the strategy he had set out was clearly not going to work. It was very unlikely that enough people would care about his new technology to support his nationwide ad strategy. The goal-setting process served its purpose here—it enabled the entrepreneur to realize that while his goal was possible, the strategy he'd laid out was not the way to get there. Be careful when you set your goals. Are you being realistic?

One of the best ways to judge whether your goal is realistic is to see if people have tried the same thing before and succeeded. If every person at your dream law firm went to Harvard, and you took a correspondence course, time to reset your vision. If you'd like your marriage to be 100 percent romance, check some other marriages first to find out if you're being unrealistic.

If you've been waiting for a chance to state your goals and your position, time's up.

It's time for you to stake a claim, to identify exactly what you're looking for. One of the foundations of guerrilla marketing practice is the idea of persistence. And persistence best comes from setting goals, writing them down, and keeping track of your progress.

One of the downsides of setting goals, of course, is that you may not reach them. So what? If you *don't* set goals, you're guaranteed not to reach them. If you're hesitating about setting written goals, you owe it to yourself to figure out why you're afraid.

So here's your chance. Write down the three things you'd like to achieve or improve over the next ninety days. Some examples might be:

SETH'S PERSONAL MARKETING GOALS
1. Position myself as the best solution for marketing problems with the six large clients I have scheduled in the next month. Turn two into sales.

2. Market myself as the best dad in town to my two kids. Increase time spent with them by 30 percent.
3. Get a standing ovation at my next speech.

JAY'S PERSONAL MARKETING GOALS
1. Market myself as a loving, compassionate, affectionate, and fascinating husband to my wife and as a loving, caring, happy, and fascinating dad to my daughter.
2. Continue spending a minimum of twenty days each year skiing and twenty days in the desert.
3. Earn consistent praise not for what I write or say, but for what my information has accomplished for those who act upon it.

Note that anything you establish as a goal must be measurable. Vague goals, goals that you can't measure, are nothing but platitudes. You'll never reach vague goals, so you're setting yourself up for failure.

Note that all of your goals have a "customer" associated with them. In our three examples, the customers are new clients, two kids, and an audience at the Direct Marketing Association. Until you determine who the customer or customers are for each goal, you won't know how to set up a marketing plan.

This is an important point, so don't skip over it. One of the key differences between successful marketers and those who fail is that the successful ones can tell you exactly who they're marketing to. A product or service that is designed for everyone is almost always a nonstarter.

Okay, so now you know what you want to accomplish and who you need to accomplish it with. The next step is to write down exactly what your customer wants. What will it take for your boss to give you a good review? What behaviors, outcomes, and events is she looking for?

If you have trouble answering this question, congratulations! This is where most marketing plans fall apart. If you can find your way through this, you're more than 80 percent of the way there. There are countless examples of employees who were busy doing one thing while their boss expected another. Pity the poor employee who thinks her boss wants punctuality, respect, and good grooming, while the big guy is standing by waiting for initiative, creativity, and energy. Both are working hard and no one is accomplishing what he or she set out to do.

So for each of your goals, you've identified:

> the outcomes
> the person
> the person's objectives

We're almost there. The next step is to devise a strategy. This should be one or two sentences that usually incorporate a positioning statement. Here's an example:

My goal is to reinvigorate my marriage by showing my wife how much I love her. I will do this by repeatedly demonstrating kindness, sensitivity, and respect.

It's that simple. It sounds a little corporate, but that's just a starting point. Make it as personal as you want.

If your boss is looking for creativity, you need a series of tactics that can demonstrate creativity. How many brainstorming meetings should you schedule? Is a weekly update on new ideas appropriate? Is there training you can get?

Most people start and end the process with tactics. They

rush past the hard process of identifying goals and customers and lurch into what techniques they ought to try. This is a big mistake. True guerrillas understand that tactics are merely the last of a multistep process.

Once you've worked your way through these forms for your three-month goals, do the same for nine-month and two-year goals. You'll be amazed at how focused and productive you can become when you have just nine goals, just nine customers, just nine strategies, just nine sets of tactics.

## Time to Decide

You're about to discover an arsenal of weapons that will guarantee that the message you want to send gets across. We'll show you communications techniques that ensure you won't sabotage yourself by saying one thing and doing another. We know that these techniques work. We've proven them again and again, helping tens of thousands of small businesses build profitable marketing programs based on our tested principles.

Now comes the hard part: What do you want?

The biggest reason people don't market themselves isn't that they don't know what to do, it's that they don't know what they want.

Think about yourself and your priorities. Be honest with yourself about what's important to you. Then you can decide on the position that will get you there.

You have to position yourself and not let other people do it for you. When you meet someone, when you go to work, when you interact with a friend or with a stranger, what message do you want to convey?

A consistent, planned, intentional marketing campaign is the secret to success for almost anyone who's made it. If you read biographies, from honest Abraham Lincoln to driven Steve Jobs to Ron Popeil (inventor of the Pocket Fisherman) you'll see that they're men with a mission. Do you have a mission? A goal? What is it? How will you know when you've reached it?

## Don't Turn the Page

Don't turn the page, don't go to bed, don't even have a cup of coffee until you've answered these three questions in your mind, if not also on paper.

1. What's my position? I am _____, _____,
   _____, and _____.
2. If someone who knew me well were to describe me,
   they would mention (name another person) _____
   _____ as having many similar qualities.
3. I'll know I've reached my goal when _____
   _____.

If you can't answer these three questions, then your marketing is doomed to be accidental marketing. You'll react to others instead of responding, and you'll find the way you present yourself changing depending on your mood. Just as no soft drink could market itself with a different ad every day, you don't have a prayer unless you're prepared with a message.

# CHAPTER FOUR

# How Messages Get Communicated

◆

*Long before I am near enough to talk to you on the street,
in a meeting, or at a party, you announce your sex, age,
and class to me through what you are wearing—and very
possibly give me important information (or misinformation)
as to your occupation, origin, personality, opinions, tastes,
sexual desires, and current mood.*

—Allison Lurie, author and professor

## The Nine Most Important Ways You Send Messages

IN HER ARTICLE, THE LANGUAGE OF CLOTHES, ALLISON LURIE
calls fashion "a language of signs, a nonverbal system of
communication." She goes on to say that the vocabulary of
dress includes not only clothing, but accessories, hair styles,
jewelry, and other "body decoration." In other words, every
part of your personal presentation holds meaning.

We've already established that the messages you send and
the way you send them are the most important elements in
communicating with other people. But this is about far

more than clothing. The marines don't merely wear a uniform—their hair, speech, posture, and attitude reflect the marines as well. Your appearance includes your hair, your car, your energy level—every aspect of your personal presence that might attract notice. And people *do* notice. People who meet you for the first time are aching for information and will give you a thorough once-over to figure out how to pigeonhole you. Here are the nine most critical ways you'll be judged by those other people:

## Appearance

What you wear, how you do your hair, the jewelry (or lack of jewelry) you choose, the glasses you put on, all make up your personal uniform. And the uniform you wear every day sends people powerful messages about you.

This idea is easily demonstrated when we look at how professional roles are communicated. At a doctor's office, there's little doubt about what role each person plays. Even without the lab coats, the professional uniform, there's usually a pretty recognizable difference among receptionists, nurses, and doctors. The receptionist of a big corporation doesn't generally present herself the same way the vice president does. Even at a casual bar, you can often tell the successful entrepreneur from the struggling law student with just a glance.

But the uniforms people wear can be more subtle than that when we enter into the personal realm. A uniform can be less formal but still communicate a unique personal style, because that style is part of defining your position. Can you tell a nature-lover from a party animal? How about an artist from an athlete? Most likely, you can, because each wears a different uniform.

Show up at a black tie wedding in a nice suit and you're bound to feel quite uncomfortable. Why? If everyone else were wearing a suit, you certainly wouldn't feel this way. It's because you know you're being judged, that people are classifying you as someone who isn't careful enough to read the invitation, too cheap to rent a tux, or a person who just isn't sensitive to the nuances of society.

Julia is an executive at a leading business magazine. From the moment you meet her, you realize that you're dealing with someone on the fast track. Her simple black dress is professional, powerful, and distinguished. Her lack of jewelry accentuates her face, which communicates sincerity, concern, and genuine interest.

In short, Julia has chosen a position, a pigeonhole to occupy. She's marketing herself as someone you'd like to work with, someone who's smart, fast, and motivated. And all this happens before she even says a word.

David had always dressed like a minister, even before he was ordained. Everyone in his congregation trusted and respected him, and he was very well-liked. But everything changed when he decided he wanted to leave the church to pursue a career in big business. He purchased what was then a small incense company, and suddenly his suits and ties no longer seemed appropriate. He was dealing with buyers from New Age and environmentalist stores who dressed more casually than he ever had.

While David had always liked himself the way he was, he realized that if he was going to make that kind of switch in his life, he would probably have to make some changes to accommodate it. Because as it was, the people he came into contact with didn't seem to feel comfortable with him, no matter how hard he tried to put them at ease.

So David started to let go of the formal dress he had

grown so accustomed to. He even let his hair and beard grow. Eventually, instead of being viewed by prospects with distrust, he was warmly welcomed as one of them. His business grew and grew until finally he had the second largest incense company in the world.

Whenever you roll out of bed, you've got to make a decision about your appearance. These short-term decisions—hair, fingernails, makeup, clothes, jewelry, glasses, and clothing—will have serious impact on the way you're perceived.

How do you decide what's appropriate? The answer is deceptively simple: Identify someone who appeals to you or whom you admire, then echo that person.

Want to get ahead at Microsoft? Sure doesn't hurt to dress like Bill Gates, right down to the nerd glasses. At IBM, generations of salespeople wore nothing but white shirts and blue suits. It certainly wasn't individualistic, but it allowed employees to stand out because of their skills, rather than because of the way they dressed.

Here's an exercise for you: Imagine you have an interview. Or maybe a big party to go to. Put on your best possible outfit for that occasion—not just the best fitting or most interesting one, but the one you feel best represents you and everything you stand for.

It's possible you don't have an outfit like that in mind. Many of us haven't thought about clothes that way before. So start now.

Once you have the clothes picked out, put them on and go look in the mirror. And we mean *look*. What do you see? Do you see you the way you want to be? Do you see a coherent, appealing positioning statement, or are you mixing your messages? Compare yourself to that role model you picked. What was it about her you liked so much? Are you emulating those things?

If the answer to any of these questions is unclear, think about why and what you could do to change it.

If you grew up in the sixties, this may grate on you. Clothing and appearance shouldn't be viewed as a tool, you say, they're forms of self-expression. A way to show who you really are.

You're absolutely right. But the question here is, Who are you? Are you the person who people will think you are if you dress to express your innermost thoughts and today's emotion through your appearance? Or can you express that better by being conscious that no matter how you look at it, as long as you're functioning in today's culture, clothing and appearance *are* tools.

You can choose to reject this. If you do, be prepared for the people you meet to reject *you,* because you are not communicating on their level. If you don't care about their reactions, if you believe that your appearance is your business, not theirs, and feel strongly about the way you present yourself to the world, then that is a trade-off you should make.

Amy has several tasteful tattoos on her upper arms, and she fits in perfectly with her crowd. But when she became a social worker, dealing with senior citizens, she soon realized that the elderly people with whom she came in contact were thrown off by her tattoos. They had trouble putting confidence in her and were reluctant to listen to her advice.

It didn't take very long for Amy to begin wearing long-sleeved blouses to cover her tattoos. And once the stigma of her tattoos was removed, slowly but surely her clients began to see her helpfulness and intelligence.

Amy understood that the people she was working with

were coming from a completely different place from where she and her friends were, and to make a good impression on them, she was going to have to change accordingly.

So what tactics can you apply to maximize the value of your appearance? Here are five principles:

1. *When in doubt, be conservative.* Conservative is invisible, and if that element of your appearance is invisible, you can more easily focus on the elements of your positioning that you want to bring to the fore. If someone comments on your tie, your earrings, or your eye shadow, you're not being conservative.

Conservative doesn't necessarily mean Brooks Brothers and Talbots. Wear those at MTV and you'll stand out. Conservative means finding clothing that echoes that of the trend leaders in your circle, class, or organization.

2. *When in doubt, buy quality.* Many people erroneously believe that variety is more important than quality. Owning thirty cheap ties is not necessarily smarter than owning five great ties. Your suit should cost twice what you'd like to spend. Your shoes should be the best you can afford—but it's okay to have only a pair or two. The same is true for casual clothes. Is this always true? Sure. There's even a difference between a high-quality leather biker jacket and a cheap vinyl knockoff. Your motorcycling buddies will notice.

3. *Get an objective opinion.* Don't rely on your own judgment when it comes to your appearance. It's hard to see yourself clearly when you've been looking in the mirror for thirty years.

Maybe a friend would tell you that your favorite shirt is really not that flattering, or a coworker might let you know that the clothes you wear to the office are really a bit too casual. Few people intentionally hinder their appearance—they just don't know better.

4. *Don't be scared.* Being *too* conservative eliminates any hope you have of standing out, of positioning yourself above the crowd. If your goal is to be positioned as current, stylish, and fashion-forward, then one or more elements of your appearance should reflect that. If a mustache makes you feel more confident, more attractive, and more distinctive, don't hold back. Just realize that each step you take away from the mainstream carries a trade-off and be conscious of the impact your trade-off makes.

5. *Be consistent.* A critical element of any marketing plan is sending a consistent message. If you look like the cat dragged you in one day and the cover of *GQ* the next, people won't know how to think about you. Fuzzy positioning is almost as bad as poor positioning or worse, yet, no positioning.

Casual Fridays are the bane of many executives. After years of building a consistent image, they're faced with the challenge of maintaining that consistency through a forced image change.

The same principles are at work if you're a doctor, a race car driver, or a Hollywood celebrity. If you confuse the message you send, you cancel that message out.

## You Have Only Two Choices

For each of the tools listed here, you have only two choices:

➤ You can fit in
        *or*
➤ You can stand out

If you fit in, you've chosen an appearance, attitude, and actions that are expected of you. The advantage of fitting in is that it gives you a chance to use your skills to make yourself distinct. If you've got something surprising to say, for example, it might carry more weight if your appearance doesn't detract from it.

If you stand out, it's probably because you're acting or dressing in an unexpected manner. If you go to a board meeting and everyone's wearing a suit but you're wearing a turtleneck, you're sending a message. Nothing wrong with that as long as the message is communicating and not undermining your positioning.

Andy Warhol chose to stand out. His wig, his glasses, his art—they all made a consistent, coherent statement about his approach to life. Same thing for Steve Jobs. He walked into the staid, nerdy world of computers and turned it upside down in virtually everything he did at Apple.

Mark wasn't as successful. As a first-year student at a major business school, he tried to telegraph his maturity and intention to land a great job by wearing a suit to class every day. His fellow students were used to shorts and tee-shirts. The result was that rather than impressing his fellow students, he stood out as someone who was sending the wrong message to the wrong group.

Go ahead and stand out if you want. But do it consciously, for the right audience and the right reasons.

## Eye Contact and Body Language

After you've made a first impression from a distance, your appearance becomes less important than your eyes, your arms, and your hands.

Christopher Brannigan and David Humphries conducted

a study that found and recorded 135 discrete gestures and expressions of the face, head, and body, including 80 involving only the face and head. They isolated 9 different smiles.

We each probably go through at least half that number of expressions each day. And every distinct gesture or expression transmits some thought or feeling, whether we are conscious of it or not. Do you pay attention to what your face is saying about you?

Are you a caring, sensitive person? One would like to believe that this would naturally come through. Too often, though, it doesn't. One way to communicate your sensitivity is by touching the arm of the person you're talking with. Sitting on the same side of the table with your legs crossed in his direction is another way to establish that you're on his side.

Do you hunch over, head down, with your arms folded when you hear a new idea? When you speak to a group, are your hands gripped on the podium, or do you display enough confidence to move around and use your hands to bring attention to your most important points?

Danielle is in the idea business. Every day, people bring her concepts and inventions for her firm to bring to market. More and more, though, she's finding that the best ideas are going somewhere else.

Danielle has been doing what she does for a long time. As she's gotten older and more experienced, Danielle has come to the conclusion that she's seen everything. She's unconsciously adopted the position, "It better be good if you want to convince me!" Unknowingly, she communicates this to everyone she meets.

Danielle folds her arms tight. She avoids eye contact. She doesn't smile and her face says she's bored. As a result, she's created a self-fulfilling prophecy. By not rewarding the people who come to her with encouragement and positive feedback, she doesn't get the best presentation of ideas. Inventors who might be bubbling over with enthusiasm and subtle innovations that could make an extraordinary difference are discouraged early and end up folding their tents and going home.

Danielle is doing herself and her firm a grave disservice by unintentionally positioning herself as a hard sell.

Back to the Golden Secret:

> I CAN CONTROL THE MESSAGES I SEND
> AND MY LIFE WILL BE BETTER FOR IT.

Every movement of your body, every posture you adopt sends messages. Do it intentionally. Make your motions count. Make your eye contact count. Realize how rare this is. This helps you understand the power of the Golden Secret.

Remember, this idea isn't just about first impressions, either. The people you work with, hang out with, and live with are completely aware of your body language. Are you a close talker? If you find that people back away from you when you talk with them, it could be because you're invading their personal space and making them uncomfortable.

Does this suggestion sound obvious? Shouldn't everyone know by now that eye contact, personal space, physical contact, and other nonverbal interactions are crucial? Well, we may have heard it, but we probably didn't consider that it applies to us. One way to find out may be to sit down with a trusted friend and do a reality check.

Even better, set a video camera up in the corner of your house the next time you have a get-together. Try to hide it or people will feel self-conscious. After a few minutes, you'll probably forget it's there.

When the party's over, take your time and review the tape with the sound off. Watch how people react to you and to others. Take a few minutes to figure out which motions you make that help you, and which hurt.

Many companies produce videotaped sales presentations for their field forces. Don't pass up the opportunity to see how your coworkers see you. You can use this presentation to scrutinize yourself.

## Habits

Most people use habits as ways to glimpse into a stranger's real self. The things that people do in their idle time can trigger strong emotions in others.

Smoking is the most obvious example. Smokers feel embattled, pushed into a corner by an unyielding public. Anti-smokers have no patience for smokers, often considering them selfish and unhealthy. Obviously, lighting up sends a very strong signal to both groups, and it's one you should be very aware of.

Cracking your knuckles, having a nervous eye tic, speaking in the third person about yourself, biting your fingernails—these are all habits that will evoke responses from people you meet, as are holding doors, saying please and thank you, and smiling. People may not say anything to you, but they'll learn something about you, and it will influence the way they think about you and treat you.

Sarah spent much of her time in college fending off the amorous advances of a wide range of suitors. Almost every guy she met, sooner or later, would get more and more flirtatious until Sarah felt so uncomfortable that she would abruptly end the advance. The suitor always seemed to feel rejected and confused, and Sarah was disconcerted and embarrassed.

This went on for several years until a friend pointed something out. Sarah had an unusual habit: Every time someone said something funny, offbeat, or even risqué, she'd wink her right eye. She was doing it unconsciously, but in most parts of this country, that meant one thing. People assumed that she was flirting.

As soon as Sarah learned about the winking, she made a conscious effort to become aware of it. She watched herself in the mirror and discovered what the winking felt like. She stopped it and her problem was relieved.

What habits do you have? Next time you're having coffee with a friend, sitting at your desk, or out at some party, try to be extra self-conscious. Pay attention to what your hands are doing. Pay attention to what your face is doing. Are you biting your lip? Are you drumming on the table? Crossing your arms?

How are the people you're with responding to you? If you're standing at a party with your hands in your pockets, is anyone coming over to talk to you? What happens if you take them out and make an effort to smile and relax?

## Speech

Here's a sentence with nine words in it. What does it mean?

I didn't tell you she fired him for stealing.

If you emphasize different words, it can mean totally different things. For example:

*I* didn't tell you she fired him for stealing.
**He was fired for stealing, but you must have heard it from someone else.**

I didn't tell *you* she fired him for stealing.
**I told Bob that Harris was fired; I didn't tell you.**

I didn't tell you *she* fired him for stealing.
**She didn't fire him, someone else did.**

I didn't tell you she fired *him* for stealing.
**It wasn't Harris! It was Bob.**

I didn't tell you she fired him for *stealing*.
**He got caught for insider trading, not stealing.**


How you say something is often as important as what you say. When you speak to someone in person, the words you say only count for 7 percent of the impression you make. The other 93 percent comes from how you say those words.

You can talk quickly or slowly. You can be loud or quiet. Use a boring monotone or constantly interrupt yourself with exclamation marks. Speak with authority or always sound like you're asking a question.

People read a lot into the way you communicate. If your grammar is poor or you're constantly including *y'know*, *okay*, *like*, or *umm* into your sentences, you won't have the impact you'd have otherwise.

Eight all-too-common speaking mannerisms make you stand out in a way that we don't think you'd want to stand out:

1. interrupting
2. speaking too loudly or too softly
3. speaking too rapidly or too slowly
4. using incomplete sentences without endings
5. saying the word "I" too much
6. having an extreme accent
7. using bad grammar
8. using placeholders like *um* or *y'know*

In a furniture chain of six stores, Rob outsold every salesperson. His sales figures became legendary throughout the
organization. To get a bead on what Rob was doing right,
the president of the company invited all the other salespeople to monitor Rob—to visit his store and listen to him
make a sales presentation. Was he using certain magic
words and phrases? Was he exerting a lot of pressure on
prospects? What was his secret?

The salespeople saw that when Rob spoke to a couple
with a southern accent, he, too, slowly developed a light
southern accent. He listened carefully, then unconsciously
adopted the speech and mannerisms of his prospects. He
had trained as an actor, and maybe that gave him this gift
of being able to almost "become" the person to whom he
was speaking, but more important, he paid close attention
to who that person was and what he or she responded to.
No wonder people were able to relate to him so closely.
No wonder he was able to win their confidence and then
their orders.

Here's an incredibly simple yet important piece of advice:
Buy yourself a tape recorder. Record your end of some
phone calls. Bring it to a dinner party to tape what you
say. Record yourself in a private conversation. Then listen
to the recordings.

At first, you'll be certain that there was something wrong with the tape recorder. The way you sound has nothing in common with the way you *think* you sound. Then you'll start to hear annoying patterns, things you harp on that you'll be delighted to remove from your vocabulary. Will it be easy? Not at all. It'll be painful. But guerrillas know that it's definitely worth the pain.

## In Print

Imagine arriving home from a long day at work to find a sealed envelope taped to the door. Inside is a two-page, handwritten thank-you letter, talking about how wonderful your date was last night. It's filled with superlatives and warmth, written on beautiful heavy paper and sealed with red sealing wax.

Are you going to save it? Did it make your day? Your week? What sort of man would send a letter like that . . . probably someone you'd like to get to know better—that's for sure.

Now imagine that you work at a hotel as a front desk clerk. Mr. Jones, a regular business traveler, stops by on his way out. He hands you a letter and says thanks. Inside, you find a handwritten note, thanking you for the excellent service and attention to detail you've given him over the last few trips. You see that a copy of the letter has also been sent to your boss.

Better than a tip? You bet. What's in it for Mr. Jones? For starters, his service will probably be even better on his next trip. But even more important is the attitude it demonstrates—Mr. Jones probably got more out of the good feeling that went into the letter than you did reading it.

With the invention of Federal Express, the fax, and e-mail, we're doing far more communication on paper today. Résumés, letters, proposals, contracts, love letters, and even restaurant menus say far more than the words on the paper.

Imagine if, to prove our point, we responded to job listings with four résumés. One résumé was for someone totally qualified—all the right schools, great experience, great references. We printed one version on great paper and accompanied it with a nice, typed, cover letter, which we consider great marketing. The second résumé was on onionskin, with one or two typos. The cover letter was handwritten in pencil, which we deem lousy marketing.

The third résumé was for someone hardly qualified. It was marginal in almost every respect. We created two versions of this résumé. One was professionally typed, neat, and clean. The fourth résumé was similar to many we've seen—poorly typed on onionskin, with a typo or two sprinkled in for good measure.

If we sent the four résumés (under four names) to 100 advertisers in the New York area and then waited for replies, here's how many callbacks we would probably get:

- ➤ Great résumé, great marketing: 24
- ➤ Great résumé, lousy marketing: 6
- ➤ Lousy résumé, great marketing: 7
- ➤ Lousy résumé, lousy marketing: 0

As you can imagine, great marketing alone doesn't get you to number one. But a great product with lousy marketing is even worse.

Here's a print checklist. Consider these factors when you review the identity you're projecting to the world in print:

➤ **Spelling.** Have you had someone else double-check your work? Did you double-check the recipient's name and address?

➤ **Paper.** Is it the best you can afford? It should be.

➤ **Printer.** The quality of your printing is very important if you're trying to convey a professional image. The type should be clear and easily legible.

➤ **Color and Fonts.** If you're not sure that you're a great designer, skip them. They often make the finished product look like a grade school project.

➤ **Faxes.** Ask a friend to see a fax you sent him. Is it clear? Is the type readable? Pay attention to any picture or epigrams on your cover sheet. Do they enhance your message?

➤ **Envelopes.** Would you open it?

➤ **Stamps.** A stamp is more effective and certainly more personal than a postage meter imprint most of the time. Be sure yours are clean and on straight. A favorite guerrilla tip: Go to a numismatics (stamp collecting) store and buy some thirty- or forty-year-old stamps. They're still valid, and they'll make your mail stand out.

➤ **Type.** Find someone successful and copy his typeface.

➤ **Handwriting.** If you don't have excellent penmanship, don't use handwriting. If you're close, learn to do it better.

➤ **Business Cards.** Is your business card heavy or flimsy? Consider the message a flimsy card sends—is it the one you're after? Photo cards work in one or two professions (real estate) but are considered tacky in most.

➤ **Brochures.** These are dynamite if they're good-looking and filled with fascinating details. But most people produce brochures that actually work against them. Check out new computer software that makes it easy to produce first-class brochures.

Investigating the tools we describe following this chapter, you'll discover dozens of ways you can make yourself look good on paper.

## Goals

*The future is something which everyone reaches at the rate of sixty minutes an hour, whatever he does, whoever he be.*
—C. S. Lewis

How do your goals influence the way you market yourself? After all, can wanting to get married or get your art in a gallery or become a millionaire by forty possibly influence the first impression you make or the long-term relationships you build?

Absolutely. If you have goals, if you've written them down, it will show in everything you do.

Every interaction you have will reflect the goals you've set. If your goals are too ambitious, your nervousness and fear of failure will show through. If you have no goals, your aimlessness will come through in your passivity.

Do you have to share your goals with everyone? No. People are willing to respond to the marketing efforts you make just because your ambition and enthusiasm will rub off. If they would benefit through your achieving this goal, though, you'll do better if you share some of your vision.

A salesman trying to make a monthly quota, for example, is ill-advised to tell his customer that he needs this sale to hit his bonus. But if he can visualize that bonus, if he can see it and taste it, there's no question that his enthusiasm will be communicated through his sales pitch.

Apple Computer had a goal. They wanted to save the world from DOS, from IBM, from Microsoft. Their market-

ing communicated that goal and they became the most popular computers ever sold. When the goal became muddy
and wasn't replaced by a new one, the success story faltered.

Do you have a goal? Does it offer benefits to those who
know you and work with you? Do your spouse and family
benefit from your goal? If you can show that to the world,
you'll reach new heights.

## Attitude

After the initial flash of your appearance wears off, what
really becomes apparent is your attitude. In a survey in
which we asked more than 25,000 top executives what mattered most in their employees, we discovered that virtually
all the attributes described were attitudes, not things you
are born with. Your coworkers, friends, family, and employers want someone who's got a great attitude, someone
who's motivated to do great things.

You can't fake it. Either you're enthusiastic, motivated,
optimistic, helpful, engaged, ethical, loyal, and creative or
you're not. But the good news is that while you can't fake
your attitude, you can *adopt* one. You can wake up tomorrow and decide to be all of these things.

Think about that. There's nothing stopping you from
being gracious, or honest, or loyal or excited. There are no
external forces that require you to be less than 100 percent
in any of these areas. In fact, you probably decided long
ago (without being aware of it at a conscious level) that it
was okay for you to be a little grouchy to your spouse, to
take a few office supplies, or not to speak up in meetings.

If you decide to be an energetic, caring, generous, honest
person, you should go ahead and project that. And then
you must live it. To communicate it and not follow through

is a promise broken. It's unethical. And it will destroy your relationships.

Let people know about it by the way it shines through you. Demonstrate your attitude in what you say, how you respond—even the way you dress.

One of the easiest ways to start changing your attitude is to keep track of it. Make a list of the six areas you'd like to focus on, and start tracking your behavior. Are you always late? Always grumbling about the boss? Slow with a compliment?

Write down your target six and put them in your wallet. Put another copy on the bathroom mirror. At least twice a day, take a minute to remind yourself of your new attitudes.

If you measure them, they will change. If you adopt them, they will become you, and you them. You can change your attitude and you can do it right now.

## Ethics

The one attitude that shows through most of all is your moral approach. If your marketing is dishonest or manipulative, it'll show. Manipulating people means using your talents to encourage people to do something that's not in their interest or portraying yourself as something you're not. Guerrilla marketers never manipulate. They can't sell a product, a service, or themselves if they don't believe it's in the interests of their customers. If you're willing to make short-term compromises to make short-term gains, people are going to catch on.

We assume that you're forthright enough to use the guerrilla techniques we describe in an ethical way. Why bother being ethical? Leaving aside moral considerations, which we believe are the most important of all, the next best reason is that unethical people are always looking over their shoulders—and sooner or later, someone you've double-crossed or deceived will catch up with you.

Nelson, a major software developer, gained a reputation as someone who always oversold his products to his partners. One after another, they failed to make money. While Nelson was a great salesman, with a smooth manner and a great technique for closing the sale, his history caught up with him. Today, few developers are eager to work with him, and all the guerrilla marketing in the world can't help him.

## Word of Mouth

All eight of these techniques lead to the ninth, and ultimately most important one: word of mouth. In a nutshell, it's not what *you* communicate about yourself that leads to real success—it's what other people think and say about you.

Traditionally, our primary way of evaluating someone is meeting him in person. We insist on meeting our doctor in the examination room, our future employees in a personal interview, and a prospective date in a bar or coffee shop. "I'll believe it when I see it" is a common catch phrase. For many of us, it's impossible to make a decision about someone until we've looked him in the eye.

As the world moves faster and we're forced to make more and more judgments, we find that we can't rely exclusively on in-person contact. So we really need to use the other three primary areas to make decisions.

Ask any competent marketer and you'll find that word of mouth is the secret of success. For every customer who sees an ad and walks in the door to shop, there are ten who came because a satisfied customer sent them. In fact, there are hundreds of businesses that have grown exclusively through word-of-mouth marketing.

Want a table at John's Pizzeria in Greenwich Village? This little hole-in-the wall is frequented by Woody Allen and thousands of other New Yorkers. Just pizza. Grouchy service. No advertising. How did it succeed? Because pizza lovers told other pizza lovers, and suddenly there was a line out the door—and the line has been there every night for years.

Great word of mouth can help a pizza restaurant. But how can it help you find a job or a date or a customer? The same way, actually. By generating positive word of mouth, great "buzz" that precedes you wherever you go.

Dr. Raymond Matta is a general practitioner in New York City. He's one of five thousand or more doctors competing for business. So how is it that Dr. Matta has a nine-month waiting list for new patients, while a doctor a block away can take you next week? It's not price—they both take insurance.

Simple. Dr. Matta has built extraordinary word of mouth. On average, 90 percent of his patients were referred by other patients. Seth has already sent six new patients to see him!

Liz applied for a job as associate director of sales for a small company. She knew that her salary would blow the budget out of the water and that getting the job would be an uphill battle. Fortunately for Liz, one of her big boosters was the company's largest investor. One phone call before her interview put her on the fast track and eventually got her the job.

By most accounts, 80 percent of all jobs are never advertised. So how are they filled? Primarily through word of mouth. Someone knows someone, and they recommend her. Far more effective than any résumé, word of mouth gets the prospect in the door for the final interview.

So word of mouth is effective. But is there any way you can encourage positive word of mouth? Absolutely, if you're a guerrilla.

The first step, the most crucial step, is to overdeliver. Treat everyone you meet as if she is going to be called as a reference at your next job interview or by a prospective boyfriend. Imagine that every client you deal with is a reporter for the newspaper. Pretend that your boss is on the board of directors of your next company. Imagine that your date is head of the men's club singles group.

Overwhelming people with your class, your civility, your energy, your hard work, and your intelligence is the single best way to generate positive word of mouth. If you are unfailingly ethical and honest, diligent, motivated, fair, and a first-rate listener, it doesn't matter who it is or what you do—you'll generate positive feelings. In a world filled to the brim with people who don't do what they say they're going to do, you'll stand out.

Dr. Matta does all his own blood tests, and no matter how busy he is, he always takes the time to sit with a patient in a comfortable briefing room and just chat.

Carmine's Restaurant in New York always serves more food than you can eat. And they always put in more garlic than most people expect—certain to generate a conversation around the water cooler the next day.

A couple in Connecticut likes to entertain houseguests. Their guest room is equipped with bathrobes, bars of soap, new toothbrushes, and even a small vase with a bud rose.

They love to have company and they make it really clear to their houseguests how welcome they are.

Tom's work ethic was to always be the last to leave the office. For over a year, Tom got more done and dedicated more energy to his job than anyone else in the office.

Bruce was a contracts administrator for a large company. He always made a point of negotiating his contracts fairly and honestly, sometimes pointing out how the "other side" could profit a little from an overlooked point.

When Bruce got laid off in a downsizing, there were dozens of loyal contacts out there, all of whom were willing to recommend him as a straight-shooting contact person, the kind of person they'd like to deal with again.

Think about it. Don't you know someone like that? Someone who shows up on time, always has a nice thing to say, dresses well, smells good, is fair and friendly and open-minded? If you had the chance, wouldn't you recommend this person as a client, a boss, a friend, whatever?

On the other hand, we've all heard of guys who used an answering machine to dump girlfriends or husbands who walked out on their families. We know about businesspeople who don't honor contracts and employees who steal office supplies with impunity. We hear the stories of hard-to-please restaurant patrons ("Waiter! Take this back, it has parsley on it!") and in-laws who make their family members perenially unhappy.

Unfortunately, negative word of mouth is far more common than positive word of mouth. Recent studies show that a person who has something nice to say about a business or individual will tell three people, while negative word of mouth will reach twenty-two or more people. You've got to work that much harder to create the positive messages and get them out there.

So step one is to overdeliver. Step two is a little trickier. After you've amazed someone, done a great job, been a classy guy, or made a friend grateful that he knew you, that's when to encourage him to spread the word. How do you do this without seeming crass?

Remember this: Every time you tell someone something nice about someone else, you're setting up a pattern for the person you're talking with. You're helping her understand how nice it is to have good things said about her and encouraging her to say good things about you and others. Imagine that you are always telling your new beau positive things about people you know, experiences you've had, men you've dated. Instead of filling the air with negative thinking and vitriol, you're building an atmosphere that will encourage a constructive approach.

Jason is a sales rep who always has something nice to say about everyone. You'll never hear him bad-mouth a client, a product, or a competitor. In return, of course, people spread good news about Jason. He's so upbeat, you just can't help feeling good when you think about him. As a result, people say nice things about Jason as well.

In a nutshell, the more good word of mouth you spread about others, the more they'll spread about you.

The next best way to spread the word about yourself is to ask your friends to help you. If you're planning to apply for a job at XYZ Corp., mention it to every one of the one hundred people who like you. Ask them if they know anyone there—or if they know anyone who knows anyone. Sooner or later, you'll find someone who plays golf with the president or is married to their best customer, and a good word from one of them may just help you get where you want to go.

When you find an insider, take some time to listen. Find

out what matters in the company, who's important, what the issues are. And then make it clear to your contact that you'd really appreciate a good word with the right people. A simple e-mail or watercooler conversation mentioning your name may be all it takes to get you in the door.

Every day, you meet two or three new people—more if you're in a job that involves working with the public. Make it a point to keep track of these people. Remember their names. Get business cards and phone numbers. Follow up within a week or two with a card ("Great to meet you!") or a phone call. If you can, find out their birthday and send them cards.

If you retain just one person a day, that's more than 350 people a year. Keep up with them and you'll have more than 1,000 people on a first-name basis within three years.

Sound too much like an insurance salesman? It doesn't have to be. Wouldn't you like to get a birthday card and a holiday card from a coworker or someone at your accounting firm or your brother's best friend? Remember, there's nothing to sell these people. You're just keeping in touch with people you like and respect. In our fragmented society, that's a rare treat.

Dan is a record promoter in New York. Whenever he meets someone, he asks for his or her name, address, and birthday. "Why do you need my birthday?" people usually ask. He just smiles.

Every year, Dan sends more than two thousand birthday cards (about seven a day!). He never asks for anything, never bugs people. One year he had to cut back because of rising postal costs. Dan got more than thirty phone calls from people he hadn't spoken with in years, all calling to make sure that he was okay—they missed his card!

Vic, a software executive from Connecticut, uses a different approach. He's a master of e-mail. With more than 1,500 on his e-mail list, he has access to top people in journalism, technology, publishing, and business. Twice a year, Vic sends an e-mail to all the people on the list, letting them know what he's up to. About once a month, each subset on his list receives excerpts from articles he's written or read on appropriate topics. And at least once every twelve weeks, he drops a short "what's up" note to each person on the list.

Vic invests about an hour a day on his e-mail list. To date, that list has helped him move up from a $35,000-a-year editor to a $350,000 senior executive. Not a bad return on two hundred hours a year invested. (Of course, you might not want a $315,000 raise and can't spare that extra daily hour.)

Word of mouth is a double-edged sword, of course. While it's a great way to tap the power of the community, if you're not careful it will bite you. You must treat everyone you meet as if two thousand people were watching. If you manipulate someone, cheat someone, or act badly, word will get out. It always does.

But the best way to find a date, find a job, find a customer, and make a sale is to have a personal recommendation. In a world filled with facades, charlatans and scam artists, we're all eager for friends to share their experiences.

## Arm Yourself

The next step is to familiarize yourself with the dozens and dozens of resources to use in your quest to master the golden secret of marketing yourself. Some of these resources are subtle—and some are not so subtle—but they are all powerful weapons that can help you communicate who you are to everyone you deal with.

Do you need to use all of them? That depends. If you'd like to send the same message consistently, then yes, you do need to pay attention to all of them.

Is there a right answer for using or not using these weapons? Most definitely not. These aren't hard-and-fast rules. There's nothing to be gained by being the same as everyone else. Instead, you need to be aware of what factors people use to judge you. You need to acknowledge that they may have different criteria than you do. And then you have to decide if you want to please yourself—and worry about whether it hurts you in the long run—or please the person you've set out to influence in the first place.

That's so important, we'll say it again: *These aren't rules. They're decisions.*

But what about trying to please more than one person? You've got a boss, coworkers, a family, neighbors, and more. How can you pick a position and not drive yourself crazy like a chameleon on a piece of plaid fabric?

The answer is to prioritize your goals, to determine what's truly important and start with that, then move your way down the list. The fact is that everyone has multiple audiences. And we all have a choice: We can try to please all of them, and fail, or we can focus on the people that matter and succeed brilliantly with them.

## Thirty-four Things People See and Sense about You

Within these Nine Most Important Ways You Send Messages there are hundreds of more pointed details and attributes that almost everyone picks up on—and that you should be aware of.

Note: These things are listed in no particular order. Why? Because everyone has a different priority list. Some people are sticklers about the appearance of those they trust, while others won't trust anyone who won't make eye contact. These things work as a *package*. You've got to cover most of them for the real you to show through, or else the missing elements will drown out your message.

**1. Clothing.** This is a huge area of marketing yourself, and whole books have been written about it. The bottom line is that the way you dress says a great deal about you.

Think about the doorman at a fancy hotel. How do you know that he's a doorman? What if he didn't wear a uniform, and showed up for work in jeans and a sweatshirt? It would certainly have an impact on your opinion of the hotel.

Frank Zappa wrote, "Like it or not, everyone wears a uniform." The uniform you wear is a shorthand for who you are and where you're heading.

Schools that have experimented with uniforms have discovered the tremendous benefits of leveling the playing field when it comes to clothes. Without obvious socioeconomic cues, students are better able to harmonize, more likely to stand out based on positive attributes rather than norm-challenging outfits.

John Malloy is the guru of the power of dress. He used scientific testing to discover what really works and wrote *Dress for Success,* which established that the way you dress can influence what others think of you.

JOHN MALLOY'S DRESS RULES THAT ALWAYS PAY OFF
 ➤ If you have a choice, dress affluently.

➤ Always be clean; it is not always necessary to be obsessively neat, but it is always imperative to be clean.

➤ If you are not sure of the circumstances of a selling situation, dress more—rather than less—conservatively than normal.

➤ Never wear any item that identifies any personal association or belief, unless you are absolutely sure that the person to whom you are selling shares those beliefs. This rule includes school rings, Masonic rings, ties that are connected with a particular area, political or religious symbols, and other similar symbols.

➤ Always dress as well as the people to whom you are selling.

➤ Never wear green.

➤ Never put anything on your hair that makes it look shiny or greasy.

Dressing for success doesn't always mean wearing the nicest clothes around, although Peter, who is a banker, makes it a point to be the best-dressed person at any function. He believes that his dapper attire attests to success and inspires confidence. He wants to look like a banker wherever he is, and his success seems to indicate that this is a good strategy.

It's a good strategy for Peter. But it isn't for Allan. Allan runs a chain of video stores and conducts weekly sales training sessions for his salespeople. Is he the best-dressed person at those sales-training functions? Just the opposite. Allan is a fervent believer in guerrilla marketing for his business, and he believes in the same for himself. So he dons army fatigues when conducting sales training. "I don't ever want to be plain vanilla," he says. "I want my people to realize that plain vanilla doesn't attract many people, so I dress in a way to convey action and to make me stand out. I want my people to be guerrillas, and so by dressing like one, I find it easier to make my point."

In social situations, things get even more complicated. There are so many different groups and functions, it's hard to know who to please. For example, though a seductively dressed woman may be attractive to men, a University of Missouri study found that "Women tend to view other women who wear revealing clothes as inconsiderate, insincere, and generally less likeable than those who dress conservatively." So you need to think about who your market is for any particular occasion; are you out to find a date, make a friend, or just have a good time? Because you'll probably need to dress accordingly.

Consider your environment, the people you're dealing with, and the work you do or activities you participate in. Consider the message you want to send. And design a wardrobe that fits your position.

**2. Hair.** Considering that it is totally useless, hair gets an awful lot of attention. When Bill Clinton sat on a runway getting a $250 haircut, it was front page news. Same with Hillary Clinton's do, and even the news-making haircuts on *Friends*.

Try to imagine Liza Minnelli without her hair gelled in her signature style, or Mr. Clean or Telly Savalas with hair at all. It's easy to make your hair part of your calling card, part of the personality you project.

After your clothing, hair is one of the easiest ways to send a message. Long hair symbolized the hippie movement of the sixties, just as green hair did for Punk in the eighties.

Your hair can say that you are young and carefree, or it can say that you are mature and settled. It can communicate your professionalism or your spirit.

Spend one day looking at people's hair. Everywhere you

go—on the street, in the office, in the store—look at how people are wearing their hair. Whose style do you like? Whose do you hate? Whose do you wish you had? But more important, what can you guess about each person's life and personality, just by the way he wears his hair?

At the end of the day, go home and look in the mirror. What does your hair look like? Try to imagine what you look like to everyone else, who they would think you were. Is that you? If not, maybe it's time for a change.

**3. Weight.** When a man on Long Island was found trapped in his house, unable to leave because of his weight, it made news all around the world. When Oprah Winfrey lost weight, she managed to turn it into a record-breaking best-seller. Some people care a lot about what you weigh.

Of course, this is nothing but prejudice—you really can't predict anything about a person from his weight—but that's not going to change the fact that the bias exists.

Max found that his business running camps for kids began to prosper when he took off a lot of weight. The kids respected him more and their parents were more confident in his ability to run a camp. But the real benefit to his weight loss was his own realization that people do judge you differently if you're overweight. This revelation led him to found a camp to help kids lose weight. Today, he runs four such camps around the nation and each one is filled each summer. Max had suffered the consequences of obesity and didn't want children to face the same prejudice.

Are you happy with yourself? Do you feel comfortable going out in the world each day? If so, then you probably don't have a problem. But if you feel self-conscious, if you find yourself making excuses, it's time to take a hard look at yourself.

**4. Height.** Although you can't change your height, people are going to judge you by it. Michael Crichton, the best-selling author of *Jurassic Park*, is well over six feet tall. Despite the fact that he's self-effacing and actually sort of shy, he intimidates people when he meets them. By understanding this initial reaction, he can work to put people at ease without apologizing for his god-given height.

Short people have a harder problem. Many find that it's often difficult for others to take them seriously, for their opinions to be given enough weight. One way to deal with this problem is to compensate in other ways—through clothes or speech or in the way you interact with others (no one knows how tall you are on the telephone). Establishing a relationship *before* your personal appearance becomes a factor mitigates much of the judgment that comes from a first impression.

Robert Reich, U. S. Secretary of Labor, is under five feet tall. Yet his well-developed voice (he was a radio commentator for years), his sharp wit, and his acknowledged brilliance more than overcome the perception that may be gained from his height alone. Note that despite these credentials, Reich travels with a step stool, which he uses whenever he gives a speech. Being upstaged by a podium is a sure way to send a mixed message.

**5. Jewelry.** Jewelry is the single most obvious clue to socioeconomic status. Jewelry is optional and completely nonfunctional. It's only purpose is to send a message.

A wedding ring's message is obvious. Most people, though, aren't aware of the significance of other pieces of jewelry they may choose to wear.

You probably wouldn't be surprised to see Bill Gates wearing a digital watch, for example. But wear one to a job interview at Tiffany's and you may not score many points.

A big heavy gold Rolex, on the other hand, is a sign that

the wearer has $1,000 or more to spend on a watch. Be aware of your audience when you wear such an obvious label. Some will view it as a status symbol, a sign of success. Others may see it as insecurity, a form of compensating for a lack of confidence.

That's just the tip of the iceberg. Earrings, nose rings, bracelets, anklets—they're all designed to attract attention, and depending on the person wearing them and the situation, they certainly will. The challenge is to get it right.

The best way to figure out how much jewelry is appropriate is to gauge the jewelry habits of the most highly regarded people in your circle. As they do in the Olympics, throw out the highest, throw out the lowest, and take an average.

Generally speaking, if you're in a business setting, you're probably better off wearing slightly *less* jewelry than average. Less jewelry positions you as being more serious, more focused, while wearing too much jewelry can cloud the message you're trying to send. Understand that every piece of jewelry you wear should have a purpose in your marketing plan. Wearing Aunt Millie's giant diamond brooch may bring back sentimental memories, but that's probably not a good enough reason to upset your positioning. Remember that you're not wearing jewelry only for yourself—you're wearing it to communicate with the people you meet.

A word about nose rings and other forms of nontraditional piercing: If you wear a ring in your nose (and it's certainly your privilege) don't complain if people react negatively. If you're making that kind of iconoclastic statement, you have to accept the consequences.

**6. Facial Hair.** Again, here's a category with a huge distinction between men and women. There are virtually no circles in our country's culture in which facial hair on women is considered attractive. In most cases, it's considered a distraction, and can easily turn into a statement about personal hygiene. Blame the cosmetic companies, but there's really no way to pull this off.

Men have a few more choices. Mustaches and beards are certainly appropriate for most men, but they send a very definite message. Remember the last time a friend shaved off his mustache? Everyone knew *something* was different, but they couldn't really figure out what. They probably thought he got a haircut. Facial hair sends subconscious cues to the viewer, rich with signals that vary, depending on your audience.

In most situations, a beard or a mustache will make you stand out. Find out *why* you want to stand out, then do it in a way that supports the positioning you've staked out for yourself. A beard that looks like something Sean Penn would wear in a prison movie doesn't support your position as a sage English professor. A Tom Selleck mustache is sexy, but if you are a gynecologist and want your patients to see you as more of a father figure, it should go.

**7. Makeup.** Like jewelry, makeup is a quick way to communicate with anyone you meet. National marketers like Revlon and Max Factor have created makeup standards, and women who don't meet them are often seen as being out of step. The standards for makeup, also like those for jewelry, vary largely from group to group. Again, peers and associates are the best guides for what works in your circle.

**8. Hats.** Hats are like jewelry. They have little function and send a big-time message. They're wonderful tools in the right setting, and a distraction in most others.

**9. What You Carry.** Your purse and your attaché case are the only business accessories that most people see when you're outside of your office. You can use them to transmit wealth, frugality, competence, vanity, hipness, technology smarts, and more. Just be sure the image matches your positioning.

In 1985, when Seth was carrying a wooden briefcase to work it was considered so bizarre that *Infoworld*, the leading trade journal in the computer business, took the time to mention it in a profile of the company where he worked. Did the briefcase make him stand out? No question about it. Did it support the positioning statement he wanted or was it just embarrassing flash? You decide.

In 1979, Phil was a seventy-year-old millionaire, living his retirement out of an expensive cabana in Miami. He telegraphed this positioning to everyone he saw by carrying a small hand purse wherever he went. While the purse was certainly convenient, it was also elegant and unique, and Phil used it to establish his status and his role in the community. He was probably the only person at the Diplomat Hotel carrying a Gucci man's handbag. And it worked—waiters, cab drivers, and strangers were always courteous and respectful.

**10. Glasses.** This is a subtle, often overlooked guerrilla marketing technique. Glasses have always been both functional and ornamental. With more than 10,000 frame styles to choose from, it's pretty obvious that they're used for more than just reading.

Think long and hard about what you want to say with your glasses. As the only thing on your face, they will quickly become an integral part of your appearance and can define a lot of things about you. Jay remembers when he first wore glasses to school. That week, he was elected president of his homeroom. He gives all the credit to his specs.

As we saw in the beginning of the book, you may even want to consider wearing glasses for some occasions even if you don't need them. They can provide a studious look, a mature look, or even a hip look should the need arise.

Howard doesn't need glasses at all, but he wears them every day. Each day, he sports new frames. Why would he do this? It's obvious once you know his profession. Howard is an optometrist who checks eyesight, then sells glasses. His patients find it much easier to relate to a man who wears glasses than one who doesn't. Nobody even knows that Howard's glasses are plain glass with no corrective lenses. And nobody asks. They just figure that he knows where they're coming from because he's been there himself.

Never wear sunglasses indoors unless they're serving a purpose. They totally obliterate any chance for eye contact. Your eyes are the most important reassurance tool you possess, and blocking them with sunglasses will certainly alienate and intimidate most people you meet, not to mention establish an aura of distrust around you. It's very hard to trust someone you can't look in the eye.

Sunglasses worn out of doors can communicate even more than traditional glasses. Flashy $200 glasses work great for Andre Agassi, while a more sedate look can make you look and feel like a millionaire. Choose carefully!

**11. Neatness.** Have you ever known someone who always seemed to be coming apart at the seams? Their clothes were always askew, tie knotted wrong, shirttails hanging out, shoelaces untied. Perhaps their slip or bra strap was showing. What sort of impression did they give? Compare this to the elegant bank vice president, her suit perfectly pressed, every hair in place.

Neatness doesn't end with your clothes. How does your office look? Are there stacks of unfinished work everywhere—a sign of not being able to keep up? One software executive in the eighties gained notoriety because he moved his office every nine months, leaving a room filled with work behind—work that took his assistants months to finish.

What about your house, your car, your garden? Friends and associates will be looking at the way you order your surroundings. Too sloppy, and you stand out as someone who doesn't sweat the details. Too neat, and you run the risk of being pigeonholed as obsessive. A neighbor, Steve, was so neat that he regularly painted his furnace, which was the only object stored in his basement. His spices were alphabetized as well.

**12. Smell.** This one's tough. Do you *know* what you smell like? Not likely. Most of us don't recognize the sound of our own voices or the odor of our own bodies.

Perfume used to be used to overcome the stench caused by irregular bathing. Today, it is a very sophisticated marketing device, used to communicate to anyone within range. Our olfactory memories are quite sophisticated, and the same way the smell of meatloaf can remind us of our childhood, the smell of Giorgio can bring back memories of our first girlfriend—without a conscious recollection on our part.

Think long and hard about the perfume you use (if any) and how much you use. Too much perfume stands out to almost anyone you meet. Too little, on the other hand, is invisible. Is that good or bad? If you want your odor to make a statement for you, use a fragrance. If there are other tools that you'd prefer, because of their flexibility and variety, then tone down your smell. An increasing number of communities in America prohibit the wearing of perfume in public places because it triggers allergies in others or because it may be offensive in certain situations. Chanel 5 is hardly complementary to the aroma of a filet mignon.

What about less positive smells? You'll need a trusted associate for this. We recommend your barber or doctor—they've got nothing to lose. Ask them if you smell. It's not that embarrassing and it may save your job or help you land a new girlfriend.

**13. Teeth.** Julie is a vice president at a top television network. She's glamorous, funny, well-dressed. Some men describe her as beautiful. But Julie's teeth are a pronounced shade of gray. For some reason (perhaps dating back to when good teeth were a tool for survival), it's a turnoff. It reflects on Julie's appearance, which ultimately detracts from her overall marketing package.

David Letterman has turned his dental gap into a trademark. But too many movies have taught us that gap teeth belong on precocious kids, and buck teeth on ignorant farmers. These associations are difficult to overcome, especially at a first meeting.

There's almost no dental problem that can't be fixed if it's important enough to you. Take a rational look at your teeth and decide if they're hurting your positioning. "Oh, he's the guy who needs braces."

**14. Smile.** Here's one reason that your teeth are so important—your smile is one of the most important expressions you own. Your smile can telegraph sincerity, acceptance, and warmth—or derision, sarcasm, and hostility.

If you've ever smiled at a baby, you know how ingrained our reaction to this simple gesture is. A four-month-old certainly hasn't been trained to understand the difference between a frown and a smile. But give her a big smile and you'll notice that she smiles back, and if you're lucky, gives you a laugh.

You've been using your smile for years, and you may not even realize it.

Here's an important exercise: Put a small mirror next to your phone at home and at work. While you're talking to people, watch your expression in the mirror. You'll discover that talking with a smile is a habit that's easy to learn, and the results can be astonishing. Experts tell us that people can actually "hear" a smile over the phone. And what do you suppose is one of the most common words used in computer online communication? It's not even a word. It's a combination of punctuation marks called a "smiley." Here's one for you: : - )

Take a minute to think about what your facial expression is right now. Are you projecting the emotion you feel inside? Do you express your feelings accurately, or is your face usually deadpan? When you talk with someone, does your face help you? Some people have developed the ability to hide their emotions, afraid that anything but a poker face is inappropriate.

A forced smile is worse than no smile at all. It comes across as cynical and insincere and will inevitably hinder your message. If you're not comfortable with your smile, find a friend, set up a video camera, and practice. Think about events that made you happy. Experiment with different ways of holding your face—do your teeth show? Do your eyes crinkle? Ask your friend for feedback.

Some people rarely smile. Though they may feel their sobriety earns them trust and respect, even a funeral director and a sheriff can gain credibility by contributing a genuine smile at the appropriate time.

**15. Laugh.** Remember Arnold, one of the *Welcome Back, Kotter* Sweathogs? Twenty years later, he's remembered as the guy with the horrible laugh.

Just as your smile is a subtle way to show your feelings, your laugh is a more abrupt way to do so.

Alex is a lawyer in private practice. He's honest, ethical, and diligent. But his laugh is too loud. It's forced. It's not honest. When a client makes a joke, Alex's laugh can be heard throughout the office. And it sends a message of insincerity—it's not the laugh we expect of a flexible, happy person.

Can Alex change his laugh? Of course he can. If he can listen to his laugh objectively and compare it to that of other people, he'll realize that he's sabotaging his relationships. The rest is easy.

**16. Eye Contact.** This is a genetic thing. Dogs, lions, monkeys, even snakes—they all rely on eye contact to determine threats, hierarchy, and relationships.

Many people have trouble with eye contact. For whatever reason, it's difficult to meet and hold someone else's gaze. Yet an effective marketer knows that this is a critical skill, one that's worth learning.

The first step is to make eye contact with animals and children. It's nonthreatening, and with practice, most people can master it.

Second, make eye contact in the mirror. Spend time looking at yourself.

Third, work with relatives or your spouse. Again, it takes practice. Don't expect to overcome a lifetime habit in a few hours.

Finally, work your way up to the people you have the most trouble making eye contact with.

And it's worth repeating—don't wear sunglasses when you're meeting someone. The information that's lost through a lack of eye contact won't help you create a positive connection.

**17. Gait.** We love the word *stride*. When you read, "They saw Frank stride into the room," it evokes a very vivid image. People who stride have confidence. They believe in themselves. They're on a mission. Clint Eastwood strides. Darth Vader strides. Janet Reno strides.

How do you walk? Are you tentative? Meg, a banker, always walks two or three steps behind anyone she's with. It doesn't matter how fast or slow the group is walking— Meg can never manage to catch up. While her signals are subtle, once someone has walked with her it's fairly obvious that she's indicating she's not capable of keeping up, or as being too timid to take the lead.

In a group in which you're the senior member, walking slowly is a sign of power, a way to communicate your stature by making others walk with you. If you're out with friends, walking *with* them indicates that you are, well, with them—while walking ahead may make you seem arrogant or even contemptuous.

Your gait is driven by where you are, as well. Striding through a fancy restaurant to the men's room doesn't establish you as dignified, it makes it look like you're in a big hurry. And striding out of a lecture hall or concert might very well appear panicky or rude.

**18. Posture.** Your whole life, your mom has been asking you to stand up straight. Why? Because most of us associate a hunched-over posture with weariness, with someone unable to shoulder his burden.

Do you sit up straighter in the presence of some people? Do some tasks lead you to slouch down in your seat? And when you do slouch, doesn't your mood slouch as well? If the way you hold yourself can affect your own mood and spirit, think about what it could do to others'.

Have you ever met an actor, a soldier, or a ballerina? Their posture communicates an awful lot about them—a sense of freedom or alertness or discipline, depending on how they're holding themselves.

The Alexander Technique is a nationally recognized program for dancers, singers, and others who use their body in their work. In just a few sessions, an Alexander instructor can make you aware of your posture. He can discover where you "hold" yourself in a negative posture, and how to free yourself to stand straighter, walk better, and feel better at the end of the day.

If you don't look as good at the end of the day as you do in the morning, it's worth a visit or two to an Alexander teacher to identify what your posture is saying about you—to others, as well as yourself.

**19. Tone of Voice.** How does your dog know when you're yelling at her? She doesn't understand English. But she does understand your tone of voice. You can use the same tone of voice to make a three-year-old cry. Do you ever use that tone of voice with adults? Why?

Your tone of voice carries just as much content as the words you say. Have you ever yelled at a friend or co-worker? Snapped at them? Were you reacting or responding?

There are very few occasions where raising your voice or scolding someone is the best response. Instead, these moments position you as out of control, uncaring and willing to inflict emotional pain on people you should care about.

Here's a first step toward regulating this behavior: The next time you want to yell, whisper instead. Go ahead. Try it. A whisper will convey the importance of your statement, without tripping an adrenaline rush and defensive posture in the person you're addressing.

Your tone of voice can indicate a great deal about your positioning even when you're not yelling. Do you sound bored when someone makes a presentation to you? When your husband tells you about his day at work, does your voice betray your boredom?

Nowhere is this more important than on the telephone. With no other clues on which to rely, the person you're speaking with will gain all her knowledge from your tone of voice. If you sound confident, excited, and motivated, that will come through.

**20. Handwriting.** Does anyone write anymore? With the hegemony of the word processor, many of us have lost the art of handwriting. Seth probably never had it. Seth's writing is more of a scrawl, an indication that his mind is working faster than his hand can keep up. It's virtually impossible to read, and it shows a carelessness and sloppiness that he'd rather not use to position himself. So he's abandoned handwriting altogether.

If your writing isn't *totally* helpless, it's worth considering improving it. A handwritten note still counts much more than a typewritten one, and the recipient will be carefully examining your writing for clues about your personality. Do you put a little heart over your *i*? Are the letters big and childish, or very small and cramped?

Handwriting experts have invented thousands of nonsensical principles about reviewing a person's signature and handwriting style. While most of us wouldn't use this kind of analysis scientifically, the fact that people believe that handwriting sends a signal should be enough to encourage you to do something about yours.

While you can use a computer to replace your handwriting, you still have to sign your name. In Hong Kong, successful businessmen use a chop, a special rubber stamp that augments or replaces a signature. You can spend thousands of dollars on a chop, with impressive expensive ones positioning you as a person of substance.

Is it worth adjusting your signature? Take a look at it and think about what it says about you. Is it large and playful? Too dominant? Clear and to the point? It's easy to dismiss this as counting the angels on the head of a pin, but a typed letter offers very few clues about the personality of the sender, and the signature is one. Think twice about the ink you use as well. Violet ink positions you, as do a lot of blots and spills.

**21. Spelling.** Too bad we're becoming illiterate. One headhunter we know estimates that one out of four résumés she receives for jobs that pay more than $100,000 a year contains at least one spelling error. To those of us who recognize these errors, this is a shortcut to the wastebasket. Bad spelling tells the reader two things: You're careless, and you're not sophisticated enough to hide it.

In a world filled with computerized spell checkers, there's no longer any excuse to spell words incorrectly. "Alot," "seperate," "ice tea" and other common misspellings should be purged from your writing. The worst kind are found in "fancy" words—the million-dollar words you add to your writing to appear smart. Misspell those and you end up slipping on your own banana peel.

**22. Business Card.** Do you know anyone without a business card? Ministers carry them, as do airline flight attendants, secretaries, and musicians. Your business card is a low-cost way to position yourself—and you can do it in two methods:

➤ *Subtle cues:* The quality of cards can vary widely. The type of printing, choice of typeface, paper thickness, number of colors—all contribute to the perception of the card. Real estate agents are now using four-color business cards with their photo on them, while you'd be surprised to see a big-shot lawyer with a card like that.

Don't underestimate how powerful little things can be. If the typeface you choose is too big, for example, your business card will actually look *less* professional, and it will certainly affect the way people remember you.

➤ *Obvious messages:* If you've got a positioning statement, and it's appropriate, by all means spell it right out on your card. If you want people to think of you as a modern Catholic priest concerned with today's issues, why not write it down?

Seth's real estate broker has a great positioning statement, and if she were so inclined, she could put it right on her card. *We sell more houses in this neighborhood than anyone else.* No one who gets her card will wonder about what she does, where she does it, and why she should be your broker. Jay's Internet consultant has a business card that doubles as a brochure and lists all the services offered. He hands it to people and they say, "Oh, I didn't know that you design Web pages, too!"

**23. Stationery.** This applies to the stationery you use at work as well as your personal stationery. You *do* have personal stationery, don't you? What else are you using for all those handwritten letters you're mailing to keep in touch with people?

When you send someone a letter, you're sending a piece of yourself. It's a piece that the recipient can hold, a piece that you can't take back. Without you there in person to augment, correct, and have a dialogue about who you are and what you want, your stationery has to stand in for you.

You've probably felt your heart tremble when you received a scented, handwritten note from a potential lover, or the fear that a lawyer's engraved stationery can evoke if you're involved in a litigation. The IRS reserves a special envelope for audits, and high school students live in a state of constant anxiety when they're waiting for those college acceptance or rejection letters.

Put some consideration into deciding which envelope to use. Personal notes should look personal—you don't want to end up in the junk pile. If you need to use a computer to write your notes, be careful about using those little sticky labels for addresses. They're so similar to those used by junk mailers that the tone of voice of your letter is all wrong before it's even opened.

Be prepared to spend some money on your stationery and it will definitely pay off. A letter is a cheap (less than 50 cents, counting postage) way to make a great impression, and cutting corners with less than terrific stationery is a mistake.

Seth knows one guerrilla who collects picture postcards wherever she goes. When she needs to send a personal note, a thank you, or an inquiry, she puts it on the back of a card which displays a beach scene, a Las Vegas hotel, or some Hawaiian volcano on the other side. The postcards are inexpensive, personal, memorable, and easy. Jay's travel agent sends all his correspondence on postcards featuring destinations that he recommends.

**24. Car.** If people didn't judge us by our cars, most of us would be driving Honda Civics. The auto industry has spent nearly one hundred years advertising the psychographic benefits of one car over another, and we've been indoctrinated.

If we see a bright purple Cadillac, with fins, driving down the main street of a city, most of us jump to the conclusion about the profession of the garish dude driving. That same car would be out of place in the driveway of the town's funeral director.

Drive too nice a car, and your friends and neighbors will wonder. Of course it's your privilege to drive whatever car you can afford, and all of us allocate our money differently. But cars, as much as anything else you can buy, telegraph your professional and social status. The make, the model, the condition, and whether you've had it washed lately— all make an impression on others' judgments of the driver. Driving a junked up 1963 Corvair may help you save money for your kid's education, but what does it say to your friends, clients, prospects, and coworkers?

Don't forget about the inside of the car! Picking up an old friend or a client at the airport is like letting her into your home. Is it neat? Is there dried gum stuck to the dashboard?

Finally, don't ignore the single greatest positioning-to-strangers device ever devised: the bumper sticker! Do you have any? Take a look at the back of your car and decide if it's really such a good idea to park yourself in the office parking lot with the proclamation, "A bad day of fishing is better than a good day at work."

**25. Office.** We're talking about the whole package—the neighborhood, the parking lot, the building, the lobby, the size of your company's space, the size and location of your space.

It's not unusual for companies to rent conference room space in fancy buildings in expensive downtown locations. The showplace space helps position the company and get things off on the right foot with new or prospective clients. Some companies, like Sony, have gone much further. Sony's headquarters in New York features a sushi bar that seats only ten people—built at such extravagant expense that it costs them about $1,000 for every lunch they serve there. Ridiculous? Certainly. But having visited their facilities, we can confirm that it certainly positions them as a company of nearly unlimited resources.

So how does this affect you? You're not Peter Guber or some hotshot Wall Street tycoon. In fact, an office is even more important for someone with a more prosaic background. People you hope to work with are looking for clues, for ways to peg you—can they trust you? Will working with you be worthwhile?

Liz is a small-town real estate broker in a suburb of New York. But her office is filled with testimonials, articles from *The New York Times* and even drawings from local kids. It's clear that she's a serious player in the market, and that dealing with her is the safe thing to do. Two blocks down the street, another broker struggles, working out of a dingy, dark office.

Office details matter. You'd probably feel even more uncomfortable than usual if your dentist's office had a leaky roof. When you visit a bank, those high marble walls make a statement about stability. Think about all the professionals you deal with. The lawyers, doctors, and even your children's math tutor. The message they send through their surroundings counts.

If you work for a company, most of this is out of your control. Your boss doesn't ask you where to put the building, or how to decorate the lobby. She probably doesn't even ask you where you want your cubicle.

You do have control over one important aspect, though. You can decorate your desk, and probably, your walls.

What you keep on your desk sends a signal to coworkers and to visitors. Is it filled with executive toys? Last week's lunch wrappers? A big bowl of candy for visitors? Or is your desk clean, with two small piles of ongoing work?

Some wags have said that a clean desk is the sign of a cluttered mind, but most of us don't believe it. If your accountant is swamped with disorderly stacks of papers, you're going to hesitate before leaving your receipts with him. If the woman in accounts payable can't take a few minutes to file her papers, you wonder if she's going to get next week's payroll out on time.

Go into work this weekend and put away every single sheet of paper on your desk, on the credenza, and on your shelves. Then stride in on Monday and watch the difference. Your coworkers and your boss will finally tell you how much they hated looking at your old mess. People will be more likely to confer with you—now that your desk isn't in crisis, they may believe that you've got your job under control as well. You've been projecting an image with that office for a long time, and all along it's been the wrong one.

**26. Home.** The house you live in and the neighborhood you choose send signals to everyone who comes in contact with this information. As the largest purchase you'll probably ever make, your house is a telltale sign of what's important to you. Have you paid extra for the fanciest neighborhood or the best schools? Does your house have a circular driveway, a large in-ground pool, and a Jacuzzi on the deck? What about your kitchen? One couple we know built a $60,000 kitchen—and they never eat at home. The kitchen is a way of announcing status to visitors.

The way you furnish your house sends more signals. Walk into someone's living room and discover that they have clear vinyl slipcovers on the couch and you'll form a different opinion of them from the way you'd react if they had a futon on the floor!

Even your phone number can position you. Dan Wood, advertising executive, spends $6 a month so his home phone will be 505-WOOD. First, no one ever forgets his phone number. Second, and more important, it creates the correct impression that he's a creative, offbeat guy.

People will judge you by the books in your bookshelves, the art on your walls, the health of your plants, the care you've used—or not taken—in the selection of your decor and the condition of all your rooms, especially your bathroom.

Jay visited the home of the president of a Fortune 500 firm and was appalled at the threadbare carpets, the holes in the sofa, and the woodwork stains. Though he said nothing about the shabbiness, the president noticed him looking and said, "Oh, I've got more important things to do than to keep my home furnishings in good shape." If you're the honcho of a huge corporation, perhaps you can ignore those details, too. But if not, they probably merit your attention.

**27. Nervous Habits.** Do you bite your nails? Drum your fingers on the tabletop? Pick your teeth? Wiggle your leg nonstop? You get the idea. A nervous habit is any repeated action that when done by someone else stands out in your eyes. Most of us ignore our own habits, but don't fool yourself into believing that nobody else notices.

Think they don't matter? In a movie, if a director wants an actor to appear nervous, he can do it in just seconds— have him bite his nails. The theater is filled with great roles that are defined by nervous habits—the way Renfield followed Dracula around, rubbing one hand over another, for example, or the evil Goldfinger constantly stroking his cat.

As far as we can tell, nervous habits do your positioning statement no good with anyone. Identify them and stamp them out.

**28. Handshake.** Is the way you shake hands really worth an entire section of this book? As you saw earlier in our example about Wendy, the executive with the limpid, uncaring handshake, people trust their instincts about this rare form of physical contact with strangers. We don't get to hug people, we don't kiss strangers that often, but we do shake hands as a matter of course. This is a surprisingly intimate gesture, and worth paying attention to.

Queen Elizabeth is permitted to allow others to shake *her* hand. Just about everyone else is expected to exhibit a certain amount of assertiveness and enthusiasm, and people who fall outside of the accepted range are positioning themselves, often in a negative way.

The guerrilla recognizes five steps to the standard handshake:

➤ *Who goes first?* You should have a plan about whether you initiate handshakes or wait for the other guy. And you should be consistent. Going first can communicate eagerness, excitement, and a desire to be welcoming. It also saves you from awkward moments when two people who like to go second meet, and both wait. Going second can convey a level of power in a relationship, though we're big fans of going first in virtually every situation.

➤ *What's the angle of your hand?* This is a little more subtle. When a handshake is completed, both hands will may be at 90 degrees to the horizon, straight up and down. But few handshakes begin this way. You basically have three choices: Palm up, palm down, or vertical.

Palm up is a subservient position. You're allowing the other person to begin their handshake on top of yours. This is a great idea for someone who's physically large, or in a situation where the other person feels intimidated. Car salesmen, for example, or doctors, should seriously consider

offering their hand this way. If you're meeting with someone who needs to establish his power over you, he'll want
you to put your palm up. Whether you indulge him is up
to you.

Palm down, conversely, is a dominant position. You're
insisting that you begin the handshake on top. This is a
confident position, and a great idea for job seekers and for
anyone entering a negotiation. We find that women get a
lot of mileage from this handshake.

Vertical is vanilla middle ground. This is the handshake
for friends, for people you don't have to impress.

➤ *When do you squeeze?* This is critical, and often overlooked, especially by women. *Don't stop moving your hand
toward the other person until the skin between your thumb
and forefinger touches theirs.* If you don't go all the way,
you'll get a messy finger-squeeze handshake. This is uncomfortable and starts your interaction off in exactly the
wrong way.

The entire purpose of the handshake is a brief moment of
intimacy. If you squeeze too soon, you cut off that intimacy,
defeating the entire purpose of the exercise.

➤ *How hard do you squeeze?* Here's where the norms
come in again. If you give someone a bone-crushing handshake, they'll remember it. They'll be alerted to your desire
to be overpowering; they'll remember the handshake next
time and be wary of this intimacy again.

On the other hand, the wet-fish handshake speaks volumes about self-confidence and authority. Unless you want
to portray a powerless position, you must squeeze back with
the same force you receive.

➤ *How long do you hold on?* This last step can become
embarrassing. Most people are excellent at sensing when

to let go, but some, either through accident or intent, are committed to letting go last.

Research has shown that handshakes can last from three seconds to eight seconds. A good rule is to practice a three-second handshake, reserving longer ones for old friends.

Seth met a sales executive who was clearly in the let-go-last camp. His colleagues all noted that he refused to let go. In his last meeting with this acquaintance, Seth decided to one-up him, and make him let go first. They ended up shaking ends for nearly 30 seconds before Seth's goal was achieved and he caved in, somewhat embarrassed. The moral: Shooting for a middle ground here is probably wise.

There are a few variations that you can use to position yourself. Two-handed handshakes can communicate earnestness, while shaking with one hand while putting the other hand on the shoulder or elbow is a great way to signal friendship to someone you don't know well but would like to.

Pumping up and down is best reserved for kids just learning how to shake hands, while rhythmic squeezes and other secret rites (don't laugh, we've heard of fingers that scratch, dangle, and snap) are huge risks.

**29. Thoughtfulness.** Are you considered a thoughtful person? When people come to visit, do you pick them up at the airport or have them take a cab? Do you send birthday cards and remember anniversaries?

Ginger's an editor in New York. About once a year, she sends us an article she's come across that might be interesting. No sales pitch, no follow-up, just a thoughtful gesture. You can be sure that this simple exercise on her part has endeared her to many people.

John endears himself to almost everyone he meets with his thoughtful gesture of sending a note following up every meeting. The note is short, simple, and an acknowledgment of the meeting, whether it was a business or a social meeting. Often, the note is accompanied by an article covering a topic that John had discussed with the person he met.

If everyone showed the same thoughtfulness, John would not stand out from the crowd. Most people just don't take the time. But John certainly does. And his success in business and in everyday life attests to the wisdom of such kindness.

**30. Negotiation.** Most of us negotiate with someone every day. It may be a big-money deal with a TV network, or just a hassle with the guy at the deli about how much cheese we want.

Many people find negotiation stressful. It brings out the worst in them, and they can become brittle or hostile or unreasonable. Stand at the smoked fish counter at Zabar's deli on a Sunday morning and you'll see dozens of otherwise successful people acting like children because of their inability to negotiate a line and a cranky fishmonger.

No one likes an ultimatum. If your normal pattern is to state what you want and then repeat it again and again until you get it, you're positioning yourself as unyielding, difficult, and lacking confidence. On the other hand, if you approach every negotiation as a win/win situation, if you're cheerful and flexible, people will respond to you.

Perhaps the biggest trap people fall into when faced with a negotiation is the desire to react instead of respond. Someone makes a ridiculous claim or an unreasonable request, and our reaction is to give them a punch in the nose. So the natural "civilized" response is to get your back up and return the pressure.

In fact, this technique almost always leads to frustration on your end and a poor outcome. Consider this alternative:

Tracy works as a gate agent for a major airline. Customers frequently attempt to negotiate an upgrade or a better fare by being insistent, aggressive, and downright mean. At first, her kneejerk response was to push back, say "no," and end the discussion. While she won her point, she lost the battle. The "loser" in the negotiation went away mad, less likely to do business with the airline again, and no fan of Tracy's.

When Tracy started responding instead of reacting, she got a very different outcome. When a customer complained or was aggressive, she encouraged him. She pointed out how loyal he was as a customer, how much the airline owed him, how grateful the airline was for his business. And she smiled.

This diffused the anger. It put the two parties on the same side. And Tracy found it easier to let the passenger know that while *she'd* like to give him a first class seat, she just wasn't able to.

Same outcome, different result. By restating the customer's angry requests in her own, more positive terms, she persuaded the customer that she understood the request, and positioned herself differently. Restating the request is virtually always effective.

Another technique that you may find helpful is the obligating question. Rather than allowing a negotiation to go on and on, you restate the other side's request, and add, "If we can successfully address this point, are we done?" If the answer is yes, you've now got all the cards on the table. If not, you can encourage the other side to identify *all* of his needs before you start giving up points.

**31. Availability.** Is it hard to get ahold of you? Or do you have voice mail, e-mail, fax, paging, and an answering machine waiting for anyone who wants to reach you?

As the world focuses more on electronic communication, you make a statement about yourself when you tell someone how to call you. Is your answering message mature or silly? Do you have call waiting at home—or do people frequently hear a busy signal?

In some businesses, even the e-mail address you choose says a lot about you. Seth uses seth@yoyo.com, an address that communicates several things. First, the short "seth" prefix is prestigious—it's not something like HX4332. Second, the unique domain name (yoyo) shows that he's wired enough to have a cool address.

**32. Telephones.** Here's a challenge for you. Call some of the businesses you work with regularly—everyone from the gas station to the pizza place to your delivery service. Listen carefully to the voice at the other end of the phone. Can you figure out what company is answering the phone? Not likely.

Considering that the telephone has been around for more than one hundred years, we're awfully bad at using it. We mumble. We talk too fast. We use the phone while we're eating, driving, smoking, even walking around the house.

The telephone is extraordinarily powerful. It's the only communication method that allows us to interrupt someone at our convenience. It's the only communication tool that's simultaneously personal and anonymous. Like radio, it allows us to create word pictures (The *Star Wars* radio drama cost a lot less to produce than the movie!).

When the telephone was first invented, it languished. One reason was that people in proper society (the only ones who could afford it) did not speak to someone without first being formally introduced. That's what butlers and calling cards were for. The idea of barging in on someone uninvited was unheard of.

In fact, this was so unusual that the word "hello" did not exist in its current use. There was no phrase used to initiate a conversation of this sort. Alexander Graham Bell and Thomas Edison both realized that they'd have to coin a phrase and create a pattern to teach people how to use the phone properly. Bell pushed really hard for the word *ahoy*, which was used by sailors when one ship saw another. Fortunately for all of us, Edison won and the exclamation "hello!" was transformed into a greeting.

There's been little progress in creating effective phone patterns since then.

If you're a professional telephone salesperson, you probably know about telephone power. But for the other 99 percent of you, here are six ways to dramatically increase the power you deliver when you use the telephone:

➤ *Get a mirror.* The way you sit and the way you look affect the way you sound on the telephone. Whenever you're on the phone, you should be aware of your posture and your smile. It sounds simple but it really does make a difference.

Think about the way certain calls can immediately make you feel tense. The four seconds that follow your first "hello" immediately set the tone for the entire conversation—or lead you to just hang up.

➤ *Talk like you mean it.* When you talk on the telephone, you're surrendering all the advantages of communication you gain from in-person interaction. No eye contact, no facial expressions, no gestures, no body language, no clothing, Everything comes down to your voice. Therefore, you have to take your expression up a notch.

It's perfectly legal to tape your end of a phone conversation. So get a tape recorder and tape yourself during a few conversations. Then sit down and listen to yourself. Be prepared to be shocked. Do you hem and haw a lot? Do you talk in a monotone—or worse, does your voice rise and fall somewhat randomly? Do you speak too rapidly?

Here's the most important phone advice you'll ever get: *Talk slowly.*

The person you're talking with has nothing else to gain information from. And she doesn't have the ability to communicate her confusion nonverbally if you make a leap she doesn't understand. Without the feedback of eye contact, you have no idea if she's getting it or not.

Use silence as a tool. People hate silence in phone conversations. If you don't believe that, try not speaking for five seconds during a call with a friend. Your friend will freak out! Use silence to your advantage. When you're talking on the phone, pause. Think about your words. Get the listener to hear what you have to say. Don't pause for more than a couple of seconds, but put some "air" in your conversation.

Finally, it's a good habit to repeat what you hear, especially in an important conversation. End the call by summarizing what you thought the other person said. You'll be amazed at how often you were about to hang up with a totally different recollection of the call than the person at the other end.

➤ *Get a good phone.* Those cheapo cordless phones are convenient, but how do they sound? If it seems to the listener as though you're speaking from inside a tunnel, you're making a bad impression.

We love headsets. They give you the freedom to move your arms and get excited while you talk. But there's a huge difference between an expensive one that makes you sound like you're in the same room as the caller, and a lousy imitation that will negatively affect every conversation you have.

If possible, have a friend call you from your phone so you can hear how you sound.

Another phone tip—watch out for speaker phones. Speaker phones are usually used by people who have never met each other. They're great ways to save on travel and get six people together who don't have the time to get together.

Think about that. Six people who have never met, using a medium that's already devoid of most of the cues we count on. Add to it a speaker phone that requires you to yell, makes it hard to hear and uses "half-duplex," a technology that only allows one person to talk at a time. It's no wonder that these meetings often go badly.

There's a solution, though. AT&T and other phone companies run automated and moderated conference calls. These calls allow each caller to use his own phone, and the quality is amazing. For larger groups, a moderated call allows one person to choose who has the floor and who can interrupt with questions. For smaller calls, it works just like a speaker phone, but the quality is terrific.

➤ *Watch out for those SOHO gadgets.* The small office/home office revolution has brought us some great things—like inexpensive fax machines and color printers. But it has also inflicted some money savers that make us sound bad on the phone.

The first is the fax/phone switch. There's nothing more annoying and less professional than calling someone on the phone and getting a fax beep in your ear. It tells the caller you don't really understand the technology and that you don't really care about his convenience.

It's just a few dollars more to ask your phone company to give you something called Custom Ringing. This will give you two numbers on one phone line, and your fax machine will only pick up the fax calls.

The second is call waiting. Some people swear by it, but if you're not careful, it can backfire.

Donna is a big phone talker. She can rack up a three-or four-hour phone marathon with no trouble at all. And she does it by call-waiting-surfing. In the middle of a conversation, if a "better" call comes in, she excuses herself from the first call and takes the next one.

This seems extremely efficient, until you consider the plight of the first caller. She's just been told that her call isn't as important as the one that replaced it. Not a very guerrilla thing to do.

If you really need the convenience of call waiting, do what Andy Tobias, the millionaire investment writer, does. He'll pick up the second call, take a message, and always come back to the first caller. It lets him organize his day without alienating his callers. In fact, the caller feels great when he knows that his call was important enough to make that next guy leave a message.

➤ *Use voice mail as a tool.* Think hard about what you'll say if a human doesn't pick up the telephone. With the downsizing of American business, that's more and more likely. People will use voice mail to screen you out, and you've got to use it to get back in.

Be brief, be succinct, but be irresistible. Create a word picture in your message that makes yours the first call that gets returned. Want a busy friend to call you back in time to make a barbecue at your house tonight? Put some urgency in your voice. Want a recalcitrant deadbeat to pay your gardening bill? Try some alternative telephone pitches until you've got one that gets calls returned. Keep track of what works for you and what doesn't.

➤ *Saying it on the telephone can be as indelible as putting it in writing.* Because phone conversation is instantaneous and usually perishable, we're often less careful on the phone than we should be.

Even if the person at the other end isn't recording your message, even if the voice mail is going to be erased, you should talk as if others will be reviewing what you said. A guerrilla doesn't separate his public views from his private ones, so this is just plain good policy.

*The Wall Street Journal* reported on one particularly salacious voice mail message left for an investment banker. The voice mail was saved and forwarded to everyone in the firm. Other bankers then forwarded it to other firms, and soon, more than three thousand people were listening to a woman express her desires in graphic detail. Embarrassing for all concerned.

**33. Cyberspace.** Five years ago, this information would only be interesting to hackers. But today, it's mandatory data. Guerrillas know that meeting people and building relationships online is an effective, valid way to enlarge their circle of friends and associates. And more and more people are meeting that way every day.

*Guerrilla Marketing Online Weapons* (Houghton Mifflin, 1996) is loaded with information on how to market your products or services on-line. It is filled with invaluable tips for marketing with e-mail, with on-line storefronts, with on-line advertising, in discussion groups, in on-line conferences or forums, by electronic publishing, with your Web site, in news groups, in directories, by e-mail, virtually everywhere on the Internet.

In the heady world of real time chat situations and conferences, your writing ability is your most potent weapon. The ticket to ride in the twenty-first century will be that ability. Those that lack it will be left in the cyberdust because they'll be denied the opportunity to shine on-line.

You shine when you ask questions. You shine when you give intelligent responses to them. You shine when you pay attention to others and don't ever toot your own cyberhorn. You shine when you can use ordinary words in extraordinary ways, when you can express ideas concisely, when you can get into the flow of an on-line conversation.

Although guerrillas recognize that the on-line world is a fertile ground for new customers, they never push themselves upon prospects and certainly not upon groups. They prove their expertise by what they say about the topic, not what they say about themselves.

Guerrillas realize that it is a glorious opportunity to put their identity into writing, to market themselves, to create the basis for relationships, to establish the momentum that will help them get what they deserve.

**34. Title.** If you think your title doesn't matter, think again. Banks learned a long time ago that titles make a difference in how people respond to you—why do you think everyone you meet at a bank is a vice president? Titles are an easy, strong, and visible positioning tool.

One tactic is to persuade your boss to give everyone a fancy title—it can only make the company look better. From calling the office boy an Administrative Assistant all the way up to dubbing the Marketing Manager Executive Vice President, having official-sounding titles makes each individual seem more credible. Now, we're not saying everyone should come up with the most impressive title they can think of and try to apply it to themselves, but we are saying you should come up with the most impressive way of naming *what you do*. Why not? After all, a company that has an Executive Vice President with a fancy business card is a lot more impressive than the same company with just a Manager.

Of course, titles serve another purpose—they allow people within the organization to know where they stand. They allow the boss to market herself to new employees with a title that makes it clear that she's the boss. The function of these internal titles is less significant, though, because after a few days in a company, it becomes clear to everyone who's in charge.

So if your title is holding you back—if it minimizes the job you do, or misportrays you to people you meet, think about what you can do to change it.

## People Who Know You Well

Most of the items listed above are especially important in making a first impression. But what about people you know well? Is personal marketing a factor at work, with friends, even with family?

TEN THINGS THAT MATTER TO PEOPLE WHO KNOW YOU

1. keeping promises
2. punctuality
3. ethics and honesty
4. demeanor
5. respect
6. gratitude
7. sincerity
8. feedback
9. enthusiasm
10. initiative

You may be thinking that this list sounds more like attitudes than marketing? In one respect, you're right. Most of these ten items could easily be found in a book on positive mental attitude and motivation. But we're assuming you are already a gracious, respectful, honest, enthusiastic person. If you weren't you wouldn't be this far in the book!

The problem is that few people are talented at communicating the good that's inside them. They find that people don't really understand their intentions and become frustrated because they're not getting what they deserve. This is the part of guerrilla marketing yourself that really counts—unearthing the good stuff and transmitting it.

Here are important things to know about each of the ten points:

**1. Keeping Promises.** This quality encompasses many of the points that follow and underlies virtually every concept in marketing. Let's consider product marketing first:

If you buy a product that promises to get your clothes clean, and it doesn't, will you buy it again? In fact, all of our marketing is about making promises, then keeping them.

You go to the Caribbean for a warm, happy, sunny vacation. It rains, and there's political unrest. Are you happy? Of course not. The ads promised one thing, you got another. You buy a Cadillac. The kids in the neighborhood make fun of your stuffy old car. Your neighbor's Lexus, on the other hand, gets admiring glances. Cadillac promised you status, but Lexus really delivered. Your next car is probably going to be different.

Same thing works for people. But the promises change more often, and people don't always realize that they're making them.

The number-one reason relationships fail, at work or at home, is that one side perceives a promise that isn't kept.

If your boss hired you to increase sales, and they go down, she's annoyed. If your husband hoped for long romantic evenings and you've frequently got a headache, he's disappointed. There are dozens of ways to make subtle promises—a firm, confident handshake, for example—and once made, these promises need to be honored.

We call a misunderstanding over promises a *disconnect*. A disconnect is a common reason for relationship failures, and it's caused by two people not fully understanding what they've promised each other. If you're finding yourself frustrated with a relationship, try to find the disconnects. If necessary, sit down with the other person and find them together.

As you consider your guerrilla marketing position, as you outline the tools you'll use to communicate your position, you must think long and hard about whether or not you're making promises you can't keep.

Can you make a list of the promises you've made to people you work with? To your friends? To your family? Do you think that this is the complete list? Are there promises they expect you to live up to that you're not?

If you're getting negative feedback from people you interact with frequently, it's almost certainly because you're not keeping your promises. Somewhere along the way, people have created an expectation of you and you're not fulfilling that expectation.

You only have two choices if you want the relationship to succeed:

> ➤ Find out what the expectations are and meet them
>            *or*
> ➤ Change the expectations

Seth knows a woman who decided that her husband was going to be rich. He went into real estate in New York, and they were surrounded by people with too many zeroes in their bank accounts. Jill started planning for a life of luxury, while Miles worked at building a long-term career based on doing what he enjoyed and having a reasonable lifestyle.

Four years into the marriage they realized that their promises and expectations were mismatched. Miles thought Jill had promised to stand behind him and love him while they built a life together. Jill expected all that but thought Miles had promised to be a millionaire as well.

Another difficult aspect of keeping promises is that you'll frequently make mutually exclusive promises, promises that can't be kept to everyone. You promise your son Tim that you'll be home in time to take him to the soccer game. You promise your boss you'll have the spreadsheets for the Dinkle account on his desk before you leave work.

Something's got to give. The way you handle this conflict will communicate a huge amount to both sides, and it's a challenge all of us face, some with more success than others. There's no easy answer. But the answer you choose is very much a choice, a positioning statement, a way you communicate with others.

The hard thing to do in this situation is, not surprisingly, the right thing. You must prioritize your promises, and you must make your priorities known. If your position is family first, work second, then let your boss know that before you promise the Dinkle account. Conversely, be prepared to tell Tim *before* you promise the soccer game that your attendance is based on what promises you make at work.

If you don't do this actively, it's still going to get done. Your son will eventually figure out your priorities. Your boss will, too. The difference is that by waiting for the message to seep through, you risk it being miscommunicated. Your boss may not realize that Tim takes priority—she may just conclude you don't care about your job. Tim may not understand the value of your commitment to work—he may just think you don't care. By dealing with the promises head on, by being *intentional* about your marketing, you position yourself clearly.

**2. Punctuality.** After a huge topic like promises, punctuality seems pretty trivial. The reason it's here is that being on time is a promise we get to keep regularly. Punctuality is expected of most of us, and it provides an excellent positioning tool. People who are always late are saying things about their lives and their relationship with the person being kept waiting. "He's kept me waiting nearly half an hour. Obviously, I'm of little importance to him."

Imagine sitting in a coffee shop by yourself, your cappucino getting cold as you get more and more resentful of the friend who's apparently standing you up. Even if your friend shows up two minutes later, going through that thought process at all is not good for a friendship.

Airlines have tried to use punctuality as a marketing tool. They've found that planes that leave on time also communicate a message about maintenance, about value, and about quality. The same is true for individuals.

**3. Ethics and Honesty.** We addressed this issue earlier, but it's worth repeating. A key factor in all your relationships is your integrity. You'll lose friends, find your career stunted, and hurt your relationships with family members if you take shortcuts here. Lack of integrity is simply trading promises you make to others in exchange for personal gain.

In our survey of 25,000 top business executives, far and away the single most important area was this one. People feel that if they can trust you, almost everything else fades in importance.

After discovering an affair, a heartbroken husband may never be able to rebuild a relationship. This broken promise is so severe that all other elements of personal marketing pale beside it.

You can really focus on ethics and honesty if you choose to. You can make promises in this area slowly, and do everything in your power to keep them.

**4. Demeanor.** Are you a grouch? People who are cranky, irritable, and just plain ornery certainly wear on the people around them. We all know someone who's managed to earn a position of authority and uses it to victimize those around him. We've all lived with relatives we'd rather not have dinner with. Chuck learns a new joke each day and tells it to those he meets. It's not surprising that these people remember Chuck and look forward to being with him. His jokes aren't always first-rate, but his demeanor is such that people truly enjoy him.

Your demeanor, your ability to smile, to get along with people, to get excited and to show emotion—all these things are basic building blocks in establishing long-term relationships with people.

**5. Respect.** You say a lot about yourself in the way you treat other people. Do you scold or snap at a harried waitress in the diner? What does it do to the overall atmosphere of your house when you malign your boss to your wife and kids every night?

Martin is a doctor. Sometime he gets emergency calls in the middle of the night and has to rush to the hospital. Does he just climb into his clothes and drive to the emergency? Not quite. First, he shaves. Then, he puts on a good suit and tie. When asked if this wastes precious time, Martin says that it is crucial that his patients respect the doctor, and that they listen to advice far more readily from a neatly shaved, well-dressed doctor than from one who looks as though he was just awakened. He believes that the professionalism in his appearance translates to a belief in his professional training. He says that patients relax and feel that they're in better hands when they see him looking unflappable and well-rested.

**6. Gratitude.** All of us feel gratitude at one point or another. We're indebted to our parents for raising us, to our boss for challenging work and positive feedback, to the cab driver who drove us across town. Some people market themselves by expressing this gratitude. They do it with a smile, with a few words, or with a handwritten thank-you note or card. Regardless of the method, a sincere expression of gratitude goes a long way with many people.

If you have difficulty expressing gratitude for whatever reason, there's no question that people are noticing it. Learn to work with your problem and overcome it.

**7. Sincerity.** Of course we have to include George Burns's old joke here, "The hardest part of acting is sincerity. Once you can fake that, you've got it made." This is not what we're talking about.

One of the dangers of the principles in this book is that an unscrupulous guerrilla will misuse them. Faking your way through life works for a little while, but sooner or later the people who know you and trust you will see that you're faking it.

The key difference between faking this behavior and living it is that you can *adopt* these attitudes. As we said before, you can make the decision to be caring, responsive, and open, and then make the effort to project—and follow up on—these things.

People want positive feedback. They want to be respected and trusted and even loved. But they want those emotions to be sincere. Until they are, you must withhold your feedback.

**8. Feedback.** Speaking of feedback, don't forget to speak up. An important guerrilla position is that you say what's on your mind, that you let people know what you think. We all want feedback—if you've ever been involved in a telephone conversation during which you couldn't fit a word in edgewise, you know how disconcerting it is.

The people in your life want to know what you think. If you can deliver negative feedback with respect and kindness, it will be welcomed. If you can deliver positive feedback, it will be cherished. How many times have you seen a couple in a restaurant, eating dinner but never uttering a word between them? They're frozen, stuck in a silent feedback loop and are completely unable to verbalize. It would be much more powerful to put that feedback into a concrete form, to give sincere positive feedback to break the ice.

**9. Enthusiasm.** Are you enthusiastic? Can you add energy to a meeting, to a family reunion, to a dinner party? Or are you a sponge, sitting in the corner, soaking up everyone else's positive energy?

Enthusiasm is said to be self-confidence in action. Famed football coach Vince Lombardi said to his Green Bay Packers, "If you aren't fired with enthusiasm, you will be fired, with enthusiasm!"

Some people are enthusiastic some of the time. A few are enthusiastic for thirty minutes. A few more are enthusiastic for thirty days. But the guerrilla is enthusiastic for thirty years, and he's the one who will make a success of his life. Like the chicken and the egg, enthusiasm and success seem to go together. But unlike chickens and eggs, when you don't quite know which came first, it is very probable that enthusiasm comes before success.

A recent survey of top business executives has shown that positive, enthusiastic energy is one of the most sought-after traits in a friend, in an employee, and even in a family member.

**10. Initiative.** Starting something is important. Initiating a dinner party, a new project at work, or a new program at school is a sure way to earn the respect of the people you're with. It's incredible what calling up a friend you haven't spoken to in ages, or inviting a coworker out for a drink, can do for your personal and professional relationships.

But initiative doesn't only mean starting something—it means carrying through and completing it. If you propose a great, new project to your boss and then don't deliver on it, you're sending more negative messages than positive ones. And inviting someone out on a whim and then not following up with the same level of interest could make you seem flighty or disingenuous. Starting and not completing something shows you have initiative, but not enough of it.

CHAPTER FIVE

# How to Use the Tools and Follow the Rules

## The Twelve Rules of Guerrilla Marketing

Now that you've seen the power that positioning can have on a brand—and a person—take a look at the dozen rules that every guerrilla marketer understands in his soul. These twelve principles are the bedrock of your campaign to market yourself to others:

1. Be *committed* to your marketing program.
2. Think of your program as an *investment*.
3. See to it that your program is *consistent*.
4. Make your prospects *confident* in you.
5. Be *patient*.
6. See marketing as an *assortment* of weapons.
7. Know that success comes *subsequent* to making a good first impression.
8. Make dealing with you *convenient*.
9. Put an element of *amazement* in your marketing.
10. Use *measurement* to judge your weaponry.

11. Establish *involvement* with people so they'll be involved with you.

12. Be *dependent* upon others to help you. The interaction will benefit everyone.

**1. Be *committed* to your marketing program.** In Chapter Three, we talk at great length about a marketing plan and a marketing program. The single greatest cause of failure in marketing anything (whether it's a product or yourself) is that people give up way too soon.

When Philip Morris repositioned Marlboro, it was the thirty-first best-selling cigarette in the country. They took their ad agency's advice and spent more than $18,000,000 in advertising it—which was a lot of money in those days—and really committed to their plan. After a year, the brand managers tallied up the numbers and discovered that their newly positioned men's brand was now . . . the thirty-first most popular cigarette. It took another five years before it reached number one, but they never wavered.

Tommy Lee Jones became an overnight success when he won an Oscar for *The Fugitive*. Too bad that it took him more than twenty years to win it. From his first role in *Love Story*, Jones stuck with his craft, doing soap operas and TV movies to pay the rent. Throughout, though, he never changed his style, his persona, or the characters he wanted to play. Eventually, Hollywood caught on.

One of Jay's most successful clients built a chain of bedding stores across Colorado. A key to his success was his commitment to a marketing program. Every week, every month, every year, he continued to invest in his program until he had more than forty stores.

There are countless stories of people who have established goals, set their minds on dreams, and unwaveringly followed them. Bill Clinton wanted to be President, but first he had to be governor. After one term, Arkansas voted him out of office. Given the four-year hiatus and the long road ahead of him, it would have been easy for Clinton to give up, or to try to change his image dramatically. He did neither. Clinton committed to his goal and stuck with it.

When you look at your positioning statement, you will realize that it won't be easy to stick with it, but you must. The temptation is always to react to a situation, not to respond. If someone annoys you, you want the freedom to blast them. But if your position is one of a levelheaded, rational person, you just can't do that. When a Presidential candidate, someone who's chosen a position as a reasonable, thoughtful leader, lashes out at a heckler on the campaign trail, he can end up doing real damage to his reputation for keeping his cool.

Committing to a position means keeping with it, even if the situation of the moment encourages you to do otherwise.

You're probably nodding your head now in agreement. Sure, this sounds good. But are you really serious about it? Really? Then write down alongside your positioning statement, your features and benefits and your goals: "I commit to my plan and my positioning statement. Here's what I stand for." And sign your name to it.

One last thought about commitment. Tell people you trust. Tell them about your plan, your vision and your pledge. Don't share your most ambitious goals with strangers or acquaintances—they'll just be jealous and won't help much. But don't be shy about including your spouse and your family. You'll need their help.

**2. Think of your program as an *investment*.** Marketing isn't cheap. It takes time, energy, and occasionally, money.

Unfortunately, most people say, "Pay me first, then I'll work." Guerrillas realize that it's often the other way around. You must invest in yourself and your marketing program. If you need an advanced degree to better position yourself, go get one. If you need a decent suit and tie to establish yourself as a mature executive, invest in one.

A job hunter we know felt like he wasn't getting the important interviews. So he spent $500 and had a first-class designer create a new résumé. It worked—he cut through the clutter and got to the top of the A pile. (More about résumés [and nonrésumés] later.)

Don't cut your investment short. Gretchen, a future MBA, decided to go to a third-rate school because it was the only one that would take her in August. Big mistake! Rather than rushing into a less-than-ideal situation, she'd be much better off taking another year and getting into a better school. If the purpose of two years in school is to maximize the value of the next fifty working years, the investment of time and money is well worth it.

Let's take a look at the net present value of Gretchen's "investment":

If we assume she'd have to work as a trainee for two years to get into the top school and also assume that the good school costs twice as much, we discover that after only twelve years, picking the wrong school costs **$100,000**.

| Year | Third-rate school | Top-tier school |
|------|-------------------|-----------------|
| 1998 | –$12,000 | $20,000 |
| 1999 | –$12,000 | $20,000 |
| 2000 | $30,000 | –$25,000 |
| 2001 | $32,400 | –$25,000 |
| 2002 | $34,992 | $40,000 |
| 2003 | $37,791 | $45,200 |

| Year | Third-rate school | Top-tier school |
|------|-------------------|-----------------|
| 2004 | $40,815 | $51,076 |
| 2005 | $48,161 | $57,716 |
| 2006 | $52,014 | $65,219 |
| 2007 | $56,175 | $73,697 |
| 2008 | $60,669 | $83,278 |
| 2009 | $65,523 | $94,104 |
| 2010 | $70,765 | $106,338 |
| 12 year payout | $505,305 | $606,628 |

If you view the money you spend in travel, education, grooming, wardrobe, and personal development as an expense, you'll never have the guts to invest enough. If the time and money spent at a writing course at the local community college is divided over the ten years of increased income it will generate, it's a lot easier to realize that such costs are part of an investment.

When you set your goals, be realistic about what sort of investment in time and money you'll have to make to reach your goals. Evaluate the size of the investment, then be persistent.

Invest a few minutes now to make a list of education, the skills, the tools, and the background you'll need to succeed. Once you've identified what it costs in time and money, do a realistic estimate of the payback. In Gretchen's case, for example, she could see that Pace produces fewer top executives than Harvard. A quick talk with the placement office at each school could get her the numbers she needs.

3. See to it that your program is *consistent.* Perhaps the biggest danger facing the nascent guerrilla is the tendency to change horses in midstream. If one message isn't working, if

one position isn't generating the desired results, too often the temptation to switch overwhelms us.

Think long and hard before you abandon your agenda. And never send mixed messages—signals that indicate that you represent two sides of a coin. A mixed message is worse than no message at all, and it will always lead to failure.

Heinz Ketchup is consistent. Same every time. McDonald's is consistent, too—from coast to coast, from country to country, it's exactly what you expect. How do they do that?

Well, if you want to have some fun, walk into a McDonald's with a stopwatch and a clipboard. You'll see people fly! McDonald's ensures consistency with volumes and volumes of rules and procedures and a worldwide staff of inspectors designed to enforce it all.

Do you have an inspector? Have you written down what you'll do consistently and have you found someone who will check you on it?

We'll focus on the importance of a single, consistent message later on. In the meantime, spend a few minutes thinking about people you know who are consistent. People that can be counted on to be steady from job to job, from year to year, from situation to situation.

Write down your message. Show it to some friends. See if you're right.

**4. Make your prospects *confident* in you.** No one will want to be with you, buy from you, or hire you if they're not confident that you can do what you say you're going to do. And a large part of *their* confidence is due to *your* confidence.

It's tempting to use the power of guerrilla marketing to

sell yourself as something you're not. Sometimes the cues and signals you send are enough to get you into a situation you're not prepared to live with. It's confidence—or rather the lack of it—that's going to betray you. If you're not confident in yourself and what you stand for, people are going to smell it from a mile away.

Your commitment will make them confident. Your investment in yourself will make them confident. Your consistency will make them confident.

Imagine visiting a self-deprecating dentist. "You know, I've never really handled one of these impacted teeth. I hope I do a good job . . ." You wouldn't last too long in that chair, would you?

Even if you pass the self-confidence test, it's easy to lose someone's trust. If you don't follow through, if you're late, dishonest, unethical, or two-faced, people will quickly lose confidence in who you are and what you have to offer.

Tony was well-recommended for the job he was offered. His credentials, his résumé, and his demeanor all indicated that he was qualified for the position.

During his first week at work, before he'd had a chance to prove his worth to the company, Tony was late twice. His boss overheard him handling a customer's complaint poorly. And coworkers found his frequent personal calls a distraction.

Tony didn't perform any egregious acts that would have led to the dismissal of a long-time employee, but without the confidence of his boss and coworkers, his tenure at his dream job was short-lived.

Norm was an absolute superstar from the moment he entered the advertising business. He kept getting promoted until it dawned upon him that he could be running his own advertising agency. So he left the big agency where he worked and hung out his own shingle.

Business was slow for Norm, however. Here he was—bright, talented, enthusiastic, and a demonstrated success. But Norm looked and sounded so young that people found it difficult to assign their accounts to him. His youthful look did not inspire confidence when it came to investing a lot of money in advertising. So Norm began wearing conservative suits with vests and speaking in a deeper voice. This more mature appearance slowly but surely put him over the top. People were less aware of his age because he had defused the youthful look. Norm knew that you can't judge a book by its cover, and yet by changing his cover, he was judged more on the basis of his abilities, and those were able to generate the confidence people needed in him.

What are the tools available to you to increase your self-confidence and the confidence others have in you? Does the way you act, the way you dress, the way you answer the phone have an impact on the message you send? Make a list of ten things you can do to project (and feel) confidence.

5. Be *patient.* Here's our guarantee: Nothing here will work overnight. Yes, if you follow all the steps and obey the Golden Secret, the results will come. But you can't remake your personal marketing in a matter of days.

A guerrilla marketer understands that most people lack patience. Because of a lack of patience, people give up too soon—sometimes just days before the marketing they've painstakingly invested in takes hold.

In order to succeed, you've got to be prepared to be patient. It may take months for your marketing techniques to land you a job or a date. It may take weeks before your spouse notices the new positioning you're taking.

The worst error you can make is to rush things in an

attempt to hurry the results. The second worst mistake you can make is to cut your efforts short because you're not seeing a noticeable improvement as quickly as you'd like to see it.

The good news is that everyone else is impatient as well. And your patience will stand out like a lighthouse in a world filled with impatient people. Realize that it might take a year to get a job at your dream company. Recognize that an interpersonal relationship can take months to blossom. Massive obstacles will melt in the face of your patience.

Remember the three little pigs? Two of the pigs were too impatient to build solid houses. Instead, they rushed and put together houses of straw and twigs. They ended up as Spam. The third pig took advantage of the impatience of others and ended up with a nifty house.

Are there any areas of your life in which you would have succeeded if you'd just been a little more patient? A job, perhaps, or a course you could have stuck out?

**6. See marketing as an *assortment* of weapons.** In the next chapter, we'll outline different tools, techniques and, yes, weapons, that you can use to communicate your message. A new business card isn't going to make a huge difference. A new suit or a new attitude isn't enough if used alone.

The key to marketing yourself is to use every single weapon available. Apply each regularly and consistently and you'll be able to make a dent in the defense mechanisms of those to whom you're trying to market.

Guerrillas know this tactic from experience. Our research shows that more than 90 percent of all businesses don't use all of the low-cost marketing tools available to them. When it comes to people, the number is closer to 100 percent. When you ignore a marketing tool, you're either neglecting another way to send your message, or worse, weakening or confusing your message by not doing everything you can to make it clear and concise.

**7. Know that success comes *subsequent* to making a good first impression.** A lot of the guerrilla weapons seem like tools you'll need to improve your first impression. As they say, you never get a second chance to make a first impression. This is a critical moment in any relationship. They also say that you never get a third chance to make a second impression, and in some ways, that's just as important.

A great first impression gets you in the door. It gives you a chance to make your presentation, to present all elements of your marketing. But if you don't deliver, if the follow-up isn't as good as that first impression, you don't have a chance.

Chad had a great job interview. He landed an executive position, managing more than thirty people.

Chad was suave, sophisticated, and intelligent. His interview techniques were as good as any you've ever seen. He fielded every question with aplomb, and was ready with the right answer in every hypothetical situation.

Unfortunately, Chad's follow-through didn't match his first impression. He landed the job, but he did nothing to continue selling himself. He was inconsistent, capricious, and even unethical. It didn't take more than a week for Chad's new bosses to show him the door.

This isn't just true for jobs. How many dates have you been on where the first impression overshadowed the reality of the individual?

Take a hard look at the first impression you make now. What could you do to improve it? More important, what do you do to live up to this impression—and what aspects of the promise do you fail to deliver?

**8. Make dealing with you *convenient*.** When we think of convenient, we usually think of gas stations, 7-Eleven stores, and ATM machines at banks. But dealing with an individual requires just as much convenience.

Are you easy to reach on the phone? Does a five-minute meeting or discussion turn into an hour-long soliloquy? Do you make it hard for people to find you, communicate with you, and eventually, leave you?

Liz was a good a friend, and fun to be around. Unfortunately, Liz didn't know how to say good-bye. Phone calls with her turned into marathons, and dinner parties threatened to become slumber parties. Faced with the unattractive prospect of prying themselves away, friends began to avoid dealing with Liz at all. It was more convenient to avoid her than it was to end an interaction.

There's more to convenience than access. Are interactions with you pleasant or tense? Are you the kind of person who makes it easy to give feedback or instructions?

Terri spends about twenty-five minutes a year in a seething rage. Unfortunately, those 25 minutes are spread into twenty-five bite-sized one-minute tantrums, about twice a month.

These tantrums have positioned Terri as unstable, difficult to deal with, and a liability. Her bosses don't focus on the times when she's not upset—it's the unpredictable lashing out that makes them nervous. By making herself inconvenient to deal with, Terri is costing herself countless opportunities.

Other than being pleasant and punctual, what other attributes can make you more convenient to work with and be around?

**9. Put an element of *amazement* in your marketing.** If a new gas station with the same products and the same prices as one that was already there opened up on your block, would you rush to patronize it? Not likely. Doing just as well as someone else is no way to get your targets to switch.

People want to be amazed. They want to be overwhelmed with measurable differences. They tell stories to others about people who are clearly different, clearly better.

Nordstrom department stores mastered this. The stories about the lengths the sales staff will go to satisfy a customer are legendary. There is a story of a young clerk who refunded a customer's money for some snow tires, even though the store doesn't sell snow tires. Or the manager who sent a dozen roses to a customer to apologize for a late alteration.

Can a person be just as amazingly accommodating? Why not? Extraordinary acts of kindness make an impact on people. Romancing your wife, chartering a helicopter to get to a big meeting on time, remembering someone's birthday—they all add amazement to your marketing plan.

Amazement doesn't just happen. It's something you have to plan on and work at. You need to do it with balance, and you need to do it at appropriate times.

Dr. Trout is a busy surgeon, specializing in shoulder reconstruction. As a doctor for the U.S. ski team, he has a long list of patients and a sterling reputation. Yet Trout amazes his patients by taking the time to follow up by phone, up to five years after an operation. He spends a few extra minutes with the patient's family after surgery. And he sends a birthday card to everyone he's ever operated on.

Does he need to do this to build a practice? Probably not—he's a gifted surgeon. But the thoughtfulness he gives to each patient is what people talk about, not his skill with a scalpel.

Are you amazing? Do you know anyone who's amazing? What's the secret? Make a list of five things that an ordinary person can do to stand out in the "amazing" category: It'll be hard at first. Most of us aren't trained to be amazing. Here are some examples to get you started:  One woman we know decided she would run for "wife of the year." She told her husband and then started campaigning. She bought golf lessons for both of them. Flew them to Saint Andrews for a golfing vacation. Learned to do massage. How do you think she did in this "election"?

Or consider the boss who rewarded a top executive with six months of diaper service when she had her first child.

Or the waiter who heard a regular customer admiring the new chocolate cake on the menu and brought a small tasting piece along with the check.

Doing what's expected takes you most of the way there. Going beyond that and delivering the unexpected makes the difference.

**10. Use *measurement* to judge your weaponry.** If you don't know how fast you're going, you'll never have the patience to keep going. Concrete measurement is at the heart of marketing, and it works just as well for individuals.

Companies spend hours measuring market share, share of mind, shelf space, and inventory turn. Direct marketers can tell you their response rate to a thousandth of a percentage point. They have to, or they'd never be able to figure out what works and what doesn't.

Every day you face rejection. As you raise your expectations, as your standards in your personal and business lives increase, you'll discover that you don't always succeed.

Measuring your progress against a stationary ruler is the only way to keep on track. Imagine a plane that takes off in Dallas, headed for New York. After ten minutes in the air, it's inevitable that crosswinds have moved the plane a little off course.

Without accurate measurements, the pilot would have no choice but to turn around, land, and then try again. Measuring his progress, charting the distance traveled, makes it a simple matter to adjust course and keep on going.

But can you measure personal marketing achievement? After all, you're not flying to New York, selling widgets, or issuing a publicly traded stock.

Of course you can. You can measure how often people smile back at you. You can record the type of feedback you get. You can determine how long your phone calls last, and how many people invite you to parties. You may be shaking your head—measuring sounds petty. But, as Tom Peters, author of *In Search of Excellence*, says: "If you measure it, it will get done."

So . . . what's important to you? Do you care about salary, Christmas cards, dates, phone calls, conversations, thank-you notes, new business, promotions? What are five things you ought to measure but have been afraid to?

**11. Establish *involvement* with people so they'll be involved with you.** You prove this involvement by listening to people, caring about what they say, and reacting intelligently to their comments. You prove it by making eye contact, by smiling at them, and by being genuinely interested in them.

Neil was a brilliant writer. In all his education, which included a Ph.D., he never received less than an A. But when he talked to people, he never looked them directly in the eye. So when he spoke to a publisher about putting some of his work into print, the lack of eye contact made publisher distrust him and think that Neil had some kind of hidden agenda. As a result, the book he wanted published was turned down.

Later, Neil found a publisher with whom he dealt only by mail. His person-to-person skills worked against him so much that only by the impersonal mode of mail could he get his book into bookstores. That held him back for several years—time that Neil could have used to promote his books and write new ones. His unwillingness to be involved with others on an eye-to-eye basis undermined his genius.

There's more to involvement than just eye contact. People want you to *care* about them. They're far more likely to help someone who's willing to help them. They're more likely to be interested in someone who's interested in them.

Zig Ziglar, author of *See You at the Top,* puts it this way, "You can get everything you want if you'll just help enough other people get what they want." And in today's greedy world, you need to go first. I'll do for you, then we'll see what happens.

Harvey Mackay, best-selling author of *Swim with the Sharks* and entrepreneur, teaches this technique to all of his salespeople. While it sounds calculating, his system works. He asks every salesperson to learn almost everything about his clients: birthdays, children, children's birthdays, and other personal information.

This opens the door. It makes it easier for his salespeople to get to know their customers—and then the caring starts. Sending someone a birthday card doesn't mean you care about him. But going to the trouble to find out details about people you work with *starts* a communication process that develops into a relationship.

**12. Be *dependent* upon others to help you. The interaction will benefit everyone.** It's great to market yourself and do everything right so as to motivate people to give you what you deserve. But it's even better when your own marketing is abetted by others who say complimentary things about you even when you're not around.

You won't necessarily get their endorsements by asking for them, but you probably will if you earn their recommendations by your actions, your personality, and your reputation. People actually do want to help you, to give rave notices when they are merited. If you treat these people the way they love to be treated, there's a pretty good chance they'll tell others how wonderful you are.

Although the guerrilla takes responsibilities for his own life, he realizes that he's not here alone and that life becomes a whole lot easier with a little help from his friends. If you are willing to give that help yourself, there's far more likelihood that you'll get it when you need it. You need to strike a balance between independence and dependence. Too much of either is not a very good thing.

Walter was an electrician trying to get started, but the competition was fierce. One night at a dinner for eight, Ellie mentioned that she was looking for an electrician and had finally selected one from the yellow pages. A dinner guest, overhearing her, told Ellie that his electrician, who happened to be Walter, did the work on time and at a fair price—*and* was terrific with his dog.

Even though she didn't own a dog, Ellie gave Walter a shot at installing three chandeliers for her. At a future get-together, she thanked the guest publicly for recommending Walter. Several other guests began hiring him, too. He got Ellie's business and the business of four others—simply because he was nice above and beyond the call of duty. It's not surprising that he sent a thank-you note to Ellie. He was dependent upon others for his success and he didn't even know it—but his innate courtesy and desire to please sent a message resulting in referrals that money can't buy.

## A Proven Guerrilla Marketing Credo

➤ **Self-awareness.** *Get What You Deserve!* should teach you to look at yourself in the mirror for the first time. Nothing in this book requires a degree in rocket science. Instead, everything we discuss presents a way of seeing yourself the way others see you, of understanding what messages you really send.

➤ **Passion.** If you don't stand out, you disappear. The most positive way to stand out is to bring energy and excitement to everything you do. People want to follow someone like that. They want to be with someone like that.

➤ **Honesty.** Treat your private acts like public ones. Respect the power of word of mouth, and be consistent in your actions.

➤ **Positivity.** Expect the best from yourself and the people you meet. Market yourself as an optimist, someone who can make lemonade out of lemons.

➤ **Humor.** No guerrilla takes himself too seriously. People want to enjoy the interactions they have, and if interacting with you is too much work, they'll avoid it.

➤ **Attention.** Pay attention to details. Pay attention to individuals. Everyone is special, and you should take the time to find out why. Pay attention to the moment. Today will never return, and you must learn to maximize the value of where you are now.

➤ **Caring.** Caring is most of all about quality. Realize that your name is on the message you communicate, the acts you perform. People forget the price long before they forget shoddy performance.

➤ **Overmarketing.** Know when to stop. Standing out too far, crossing too many boundaries, being too good at it—these actions will backfire. Go slowly until you're sure the ice is thick enough to support your weight.

## If at First You Don't Succeed, Ask Yourself These Questions

Guerrilla Marketing Yourself techniques don't work instantly for everyone. Some people find that they're still not getting the job they want. They still don't have the relationships they seek. If this happens to you, ask and answer these four questions:

1. *Have you given it enough time?* Nothing works overnight. You're on this earth for another thirty, forty, maybe even sixty years, and you should act accordingly. You can't implement a major life change in a week, and you shouldn't expect to.

What you should be doing, however, is measuring yourself. You should see some progress right away. If you're implementing the tools properly, people will notice. Not all at once, and not in a big way, but soon.

2. *Have you tested your message?* You need to find trusted friends and colleagues and ask them if the tools you're using are sending the signals you think they are. Make lists. Write stuff down. Keep tweaking.

3. *Are your goals clear and reasonable?* Are you hoping to attain something that's too difficult or outside your realm? Nothing here is going to get you a date with Cindy Crawford or an on-screen role with Paul Newman.

You should have written down your goals and taken a hard look at them. Has anyone *ever* accomplished what you're setting out to do? Pursuing unreasonable goals, especially in a short time frame, does you no good.

4. *Are you being sincere or cynical?* See the warning at the beginning of the book. If people sense that your marketing is designed to manipulate them, designed to mask your true self, it will fail. Guaranteed. Sooner or later, your insincerity will show through, people will feel violated and cheated, and you will fool no one.

**CHAPTER SIX**

# *Application*

◆

## Bringing It All Together

Using the telephone, handwritten letters, newspaper clippings, word of mouth, e-mail, and other forms of noninterpersonal communication give you a huge leg up on just about everyone else.

The guerrilla realizes that no single tool is the answer to every problem. But working as a system, used over a period of time, used consistently and persistently, these tools lay the groundwork for unparalleled success. Add them to your arsenal and watch the difference they make.

## Guerrilla Marketing Yourself into a Job: Application #1

What are the landmark moments in your life? Well, your birth surely is one of them. And certainly your first day at school counts. Your graduation counts, too—all your graduations in fact, if you've had more than one. Let's not forget your confirmation, your marriage, that first car you bought, your first day at college, your first house or apartment, the birth of your first child.

Ranking right up there with those biggies is your job. We don't mean those summer jobs you toiled at while you were at school. Instead, we're referring to the first job in what you hoped would be your career. It was supposed to set you on a course upon which you'd sail for the rest of your life, or at least for a goodly portion of it. Was it the exact job you had dreamt about? Was it the perfect job for you at the time?

Chances are that it wasn't. Department of Commerce statistics reveal that over 80 percent of people aren't all that thrilled with their jobs. Either they got that job even though it wasn't the job they really wanted, or they got the position they wanted but learned that it wasn't nearly as satisfying as they had hoped or expected.

Drudging away for the better part of a lifetime at an unsatisfying job is hardly guerrilla behavior. Guerrillas seem to have a knack for identifying the jobs that suit them ideally, then landing those jobs and loving them. "Take this job and love it" are words not entirely unfamiliar to them.

But how do you get the exact job you want?

The answer is by guerrilla marketing yourself into that job, by knowing who offers it, then getting it—even though many others want the very same job.

This process begins with you knowing exactly who you are, what you can do, what type of job you should have, which companies offer that particular job, and then, how to get it for yourself—the job, the responsibilities, the opportunities for growth, the salary, and the perks.

Savvy guerrillas survey companies they admire, businesses that have the exact jobs they want. They visit these companies, setting up what Richard Nelson Bolles, in his wonderful *What Color Is Your Parachute?*, a book updated each year, describes as "informational interviews." These entail learning the chemistry of the company, their problems, their opportunities, and their needs, then fitting yourself in as just the person who can match their chemistry, help solve their problems, help capitalize upon their opportunities, and fill their needs. Who could deny a job to a person such as that?

Many companies do deny qualified applicants those jobs. Why? Because the applicants haven't a clue about how to market themselves, how to position themselves compellingly, and how to get exactly what they honestly do deserve.

The first thing you have to realize is that the single WORST place to look for a job is in the Help Wanted ads. Less than one in ten jobs are filled through the classifieds, and virtually all of the good jobs never get listed.

Surprised? Don't be. Over the last ten years, the net growth in jobs offered by the Fortune 500 is exactly zero—that's right, zero. The same number of people work there now as in 1986. All the job growth in our economy comes from small- and medium-size businesses. But small businesses often don't know they're looking to fill a job until the right person comes along and persuades them that he or she can add value. Add to that the hesitation people have about hiring someone they don't know. Referrals and word of mouth are far more important to companies than the way your résumé looks. Jobs aren't found in the newspaper. They're picked from the grapevine.

Unfortunately, most people feel as though they're putting their self-esteem on the line when they go job hunting. They feel as though getting or not getting a job based on a thirty-minute interview is a reflection on their worth as a person. But we all know that's not the case. Getting a job is a classic marketing problem. It relies on the tactics and techniques that have been described throughout this book. If you don't get a job, it's not because you're a bad person. It's because you haven't marketed yourself properly, or you've chosen the wrong customer.

The job of finding a job is a six-step process. Skip any one of the steps and you'll find yourself in the street, still fantasizing about what might have been. Take all six steps properly and there you'll be—doing the work you love for the company you love with a bright future ahead of you. The six steps, after you've identified the job you want, are as follows:

1. *Position yourself.* Write a positioning statement about yourself. Identify who you are and where you're going.

2. *Identify your customers.* Identify the companies you're after—the companies you want to work for and that honestly need what you have to offer and can benefit from your contributions.

3. *Prepare a nonrésumé and a plan.* Prepare a guerrilla nonrésumé, a word-of-mouth campaign, and a marketing strategy that reflects your positioning and gets you an interview.

4. *Give them a reason to hire you.* Impress those who interview you so much that they'd move heaven and earth to hire you.

5. *Maintain your momentum.* Conduct a postinterview marketing campaign that maintains your momentum.

6. *Accept the job and start all over again.* Accept the job offer, making certain that you're getting all that you deserve—responsibilities, money, fringe benefits, the works—

and then making sure that you follow through on every-thing you promised your new employer.

## Step One: Position Yourself

Never forget that if you don't position yourself, some-body else is going to position you—and you may not be happy with the way they do it. Even if you get an interview, you'll have about five seconds to make a first impression, then another few minutes to live up to that impression. The positioning statement you send may very well be the only message received and remembered by your customer, the employer. So be very careful to choose the message you wish to send. It's the one that will market you.

You're a dynamite copywriter angling for a job in an advertising agency, and you've got a specialization in writ-ing engaging, motivational copy to sell computers. But your résumé has a misspelled word. Ding. You've gone from being a potential hire to "the copywriter who's careless." It's not worth another nanosecond of the recruiter's time to consider you. There are too many other good people out there.

Or you're a great salesperson, with great credentials and a wonderful handshake. But during your job interview, you mention something disparaging about your previous boss.

Instead of being positioned as "the salesman who makes computers walk out the door," you're positioned as "the unappreciative ingrate who bad-mouths his last job."

The way around this poor positioning is to think of your-self in terms of the company at which you want to land a job. There's no difference between Coca-Cola selling a can of soda, IBM selling a computer, or you looking for a job. You all have a potential customer, and you must advertise and market yourself if you want to make the sale.

When you view the job search process in this way, it becomes crystal clear. Find the right customers, then market to them. Mercedes Benz advertises in *Wired* magazine because rich people read it. If you're hoping to make $200,000 a year as a salesman, don't apply for a job at a low-profit job in a low-paying industry. Fish where the fish are.

It's worth taking a minute to go back over that last paragraph. Perhaps the most critical decision you're going to make involves the industry and the position you say you want. If you pick the wrong one—a high-paying, high-pressure job when you detest stress, a low-paying industry when you have expensive tastes—you're going to be miserable. Take a few minutes now—you owe them to yourself—to know yourself, to set yourself up for success, not failure.

Don't just think it. Clearly identify the areas where you excel, the goals you need to reach. Write them down. Putting goals in writing establishes crucial momentum toward achieving them.

Picking the right industry and the right companies in that industry means rejecting far more opportunities than you pursue. That's critical. If you don't do it, you'll be heading down the wrong path right at the start.

Personnel directors tell us story after story of résumés and cover letters that are obviously being sent to every single ad in the newspaper. The overworked, harried person opening the mail can smell these résumés a mile away, and they all end up in the trash. Save yourself some trouble, and make it easier for everyone else by specializing. Most traditional job searches fail because they're too general and don't take advantage of the guerrilla's ability to capitalize on a niche.

## *Step Two: Identify Your Customers*

Your first step is a trip to the library. Or maybe you have access to the on-line library. A good library carries hundreds of trade magazines, from *Pizza Today* to the *Journal of Business Strategy*. These trade magazines are your secret weapons—the overlooked radar that shows you exactly which companies need your services.

Pick the magazines that interest you the most. The ones you pick shine a light on where to start in your job search. Read through a year of issues of the magazines you select. Who's being written about? Who's advertising? Make a list of a dozen companies that are in the right geographical area. Hone in on them. Focus like a laser beam.

What do these companies need? When Microsoft announced it was focusing every product and every service on the Internet, it sent a signal to job searchers everywhere. When General Appliance announces that its widget division is expecting to double its market share in the next two years, it will be speaking directly to you—if you know anything about widgets or just about anything else a fast-growing widget division needs.

Try to learn as much as possible about each of the places on your list. If they're big companies, you could write to each company and ask for an annual report or a media kit. If not, gather as much information as you can with what's available. Read it like a detective, looking for every clue you can find about what the company does and how it does it. If this seems like a place where you'd like to work, you've just found a target customer. You've identified one of a dozen places where you're going to work to market yourself.

This marketing includes your résumé, your cover letter, your interview, absolutely everything. It should back up

your positioning and prove by deeds more than words that
you truly are what you say you are.

Your first step, then, is to create a positioning statement—six to eighteen words that describe what benefits you
offer to a potential employer. Before you start, be aware of
what employers look for in prospective employees. A 1996
survey reported that they look for work ethic first, then
intelligence, then enthusiasm, and finally, education.

Seth did a survey of more than 25,000 top executives for
another book, *Wisdom, Inc*. In it, he found that the ten
most important attributes searched for in an employee are
the following:

1. ethics
2. teamwork
3. honesty
4. curiosity
5. hard work
6. intelligence
7. self-motivation
8. sense of humor
9. initiative
10. creativity

You'll want specifics to round out your general positioning
statement. What skills and experience do you bring with you?

I am _____, _____ and _____.
Previous employers were pleased with my _____
_____, _____ and
_____. I'm among the best in the field
when I am _____.

Now, boil down your positioning statement to as few words as you can.

Oklahoma's hardest-working oil foreman. My employees will walk on glass for me.

A visionary computer marketing executive with three successful product launches to his credit.

An honest PR professional who places stories in *Time, Inc., Entrepreneur,* and on TV.

Guerrillas always remember where their positioning really takes place. Sure, it takes place on your résumé and in your interview. But the most important stage for it is within the mind of the person interviewing you. That's where you've got to establish your position. If you don't establish it there, everywhere else you've emblazoned it becomes meaningless.

The position you select must have four elements for it to work for you:

1. It must be one you can live up to.
2. It must be one that can help your prospective employer.
3. It must be one that differentiates you from other applicants.
4. It must be succinct and easy to understand.

### Step Three: Prepare a Nonrésumé and a Plan

Bypass the résumé-screening process by not having a résumé at all. That's right. No résumé.

That's one way to get their attention. It sounds like heresy, but once you try it, you'll see how effective it is. The basic fact behind this truth is that companies don't hire people, people do. And the people looking to hire someone have two problems.

The first problem a hiring executive has is that she has no time at all for the task. The second problem is she doesn't want to screw up. She doesn't want to hire someone who's not motivated, who's likely to leave soon, who isn't what he said he was, or who isn't good at his job. Hiring is almost a no-win proposition for this executive—nothing but downside opportunity.

That said, this is the perfect place for a guerrilla. You *know* how to save her time. You *know* how to avoid her nightmare of hiring the wrong person. You're going to do this by orchestrating a marketing plan that will get you an interview by busting the system. However you do it, getting them to notice you is key.

Carl found a way to get noticed. Carl was one of three hundred MBAs graduating from Stanford Business School in the middle of the bull market of the 1980s. As you might expect, most of those three hundred newly minted MBAs headed for Wall Street. Given the glut of essentially identical talent, how could Carl stand out?

Carl did it with beekeeping. In high school, he had kept an apiary, and his parents kept it up for him while he was off at school. Carl had great stories to tell about queens and drones, about honey and bee stings. There, at the bottom of his résumé, were four key words:

Hobbies: rusty French, beekeeping

Every single person who interviewed Carl asked about the bees. His interview, jammed into twenty others that day, stood out. Everyone else talked about the stock market and PE ratios. Carl, at the interviewer's request, talked about bees. To date, Carl has earned well over a million dollars on Wall Street, in no small part because he got his foot in the door by talking about bees.

Besides getting noticed, the first step of your interview marketing plan is identifying the key players in the companies you've chosen. If you've done your homework, you've already collected annual reports and other information about the company. Now you need to get serious. You need to identify a handful of decision makers at each company. Get their names, their direct dial numbers, fax numbers, e-mail addresses. Find out whatever you can about them from the press releases and other material that the company offers. Figure out if the company belongs to an association or trade group. Get information from them on the industry and the company. You can't know too much.

Your next move is to try to find someone who knows one of these key players. Call your friends, your contacts in the industry. Ask around. Find a mutual friend, "Hi Bob. Say, do you know Bill Larson at McAffee? I'd really like to get an introduction to him . . ." If you come up blank, don't despair. But a personal introduction is worth its weight in gold.

Note that we haven't asked you to get in touch with the company formally yet. It's not time.

Step three is to put together your nonrésumé. The single most important part of this five-page document is the last four sheets. Letters of recommendation. Startling truth: What people say about you is more important than what you say about yourself.

It's always puzzled us that the most important part of the résumé is left off. "References available upon request"— aren't they always available upon request? If you've got good references, and you ought to if you're a guerrilla, share them generously.

Your references should support your positioning statement. If you're positioning yourself as a hardworking, resourceful administrative assistant, every letter should talk about that—not focus on your gardening, your work at church, or your family. Ideally, at least one letter will be from a former boss, and others will be from people you've worked with inside and outside your previous company.

> *Note:* Don't include a lukewarm letter. It has to be over-the-top, filled with enthusiasm and concrete examples. The letter has to make it really clear that you will do an extraordinary job, as your positioning promises.

Jennifer was looking for a job after moving to the United States from Germany. Faced with no network (all her contacts were in Germany) and a difficult-to-transfer job (she was editor-in-chief of a small magazine), she thought she'd have trouble. In fact, Jennifer was offered a great job at the very first place she interviewed. Why? Because the letter from the publisher of her magazine in Germany was so positive, so enthusiastic, that the hiring executive knew that he'd be a fool to pass up this opportunity.

What about the first page? Well, it certainly isn't a formal résumé. A formal résumé is filled with meaningless data (who cares where a person in the work force for twenty years went to college?) and leaves no room for the really good stuff.

Instead, write a letter. In it, mention your previous job or two, your relevant educational experience, and your positioning statement. Highlight (underline or bold) the key entries—the entries that the employer would look for on a résumé. Most important, emphasize the research you've done on the company and the focus you've put on it. Of course, you should write about yourself. You should also write about the company.

Remember, the purpose of the letter is *not* to get you a

job. It's to get you an interview. It's the last step in a long research process, the first step in the job-getting process, and you need to make it clear to the reader of the letter that it's a much better idea to talk to you than it is to throw the letter into the wastebasket.

Here's a sample:

---

Mr. Bill Larson
Chairman
McAffee Associates
123 Sun Lane
San Francisco, CA 12345

Dear Mr. Larson,

Roger Engel at Silver Associates suggested I write to you. As you can see from the attached, I'm an award-winning art director with a successful history of turning stodgy high-tech companies into good-looking market stars.

I've used your virus software and have been extremely impressed with the quality of your engineering and design. Over the years, I've also seen the ads you run in *InfoWorld, Datamation,* and other leading magazines. I think the image and positioning of McAffee is terrific, and I'd like to be part of your success.

I'm writing to ask you to set up an interview for me with someone in your marketing department. I know that Sylvia McIntire, your former art director, recently left to go to Davidson, and I think I can help McAffee grow by joining your art department.

At APPLE, I was responsible for the profitable Newton Now! campaign, creating all the packaging and ancillary materials. Before that, I created the logo for WORLDWIDE DATA, and consulted to more than a dozen companies in Silicon Valley.

My training at the PRATT INSTITUTE, combined with more than fifteen years experience, make this a great fit. I'll follow up with Shirley Davis next Monday to set up a time. Thanks for your consideration.

Yours,

Ron Downing

P.S. I really admire your new logo. Who created it?

A few notes on this letter:

➤ The personal reference in the first line guarantees the letter will get read.
➤ The details about McAffee's products let the reader know that you've taken the time to do your research.
➤ The fact that you know the art director has left (not so hard if you attend the monthly art director club luncheon) makes it clear you're an insider.
➤ The letters of recommendation attached are more important than your own letter.
➤ Mentioning Bill's secretary by name makes her feel good (she's screening his mail) and makes it even more clear you're really focused.
➤ The P.S. is always a nice touch, especially if you have a sincere compliment to share.

Ron is off to a good start. Already he's positioned himself as aggressive, knowledgeable, and involved. He knew that the person reading this letter would want to see that he was experienced, qualified, and specifically interested in that company.

The question? Do you think this letter is more likely to get him an interview? Was his six or seven hours of research worth it? Well, if it got him closer to a job that pays him a good income, or allows him to do what he loves, you bet it was.

### Step Four: Give Them a Reason to Hire You

After setting up the interview, think about what kind of impression you want to make. First, when negotiating the time and date, ask the person with whom you're talking to please send you materials about the company. Sample products. Ads. Annual report. Anything you can get your hands on. You'll be surprised at how much you'll receive if you ask.

First, have your position ready. Practice it out loud. Practice it on a friend. Write it down. Work with it until it's clear, short, and memorable. Make sure it positions you the way you want to be thought of. Were you president of your fraternity last year? If you mention that, be prepared to be remembered as a John Belushi/*Animal House* escapee, unless you know in advance that the interviewer is a brother. Did you have a two-month stint four years ago that turned out badly? Don't mention it. Don't lie, don't hide anything. But choose what you focus on carefully.

Second, you need to be ready to talk about yourself. Ask yourself the question, "Tell me a little about yourself?" Do you hesitate, or can you encapsulate and position yourself in two minutes or less? No one wants to know your life story. But they may want to know what you have to say. What you express about yourself tells a lot about you.

Be ready to talk about the company, the job, and the interviewer. What are they supposed to be impressed with? Not your clothes. Not your jewelry. Not your hairstyle. Not the funny jokes you tell. Those who have the authority to hire you should be impressed with your qualifications for the job, with what you can do for their company, how you, as a personnel pro, can make them look good. Of course, if they get stuck on the surface stuff, they'll never take the time to hear the things you *want* them to know.

Your qualifications include your attitude, your background, and how your chemistry fits closely with their own chemistry. It all begins with the first impression that you make—the only chance you'll have to make a first impression. Guerrillas make a positive one with lots of eye contact, with a firm handshake that communicates confidence and trust, with an active conversational style that embraces both talking and listening, and with smiles at the appropriate times.

In your interview, prove that you know about the company. Use specifics instead of generalities. Ask questions. Listen carefully to the answers. Orient everything you're saying to the good of the company you wish to hire you. Relate your experience to the benefits of hiring you. Prove beyond doubt that you are exactly as you have positioned yourself and that you are exactly what the company needs.

Once again, we remind you that this is not a book about being interviewed. There are several fine ones at your local bookstore or library—an especially good one is *The Ultimate Interview,* by John Caple. But we do want you to know that your greatest ally during your own interview will be knowledge. This means knowledge of the company interviewing you, knowledge about their industry, knowledge about the industry in which your work will be involved, knowledge about the people working at the company interviewing you, knowledge about the job itself, and knowledge of the competitive situation. The more you know about all these areas, the better you'll be able to guerrilla market yourself.

You'll market yourself with words, with facts, with your personality. You'll market yourself with your posture, your gestures, your way of responding to questions, the questions you ask, the answers you give. Guerrillas learn what interviewers want, then give it to them in a way compatible with their own essence.

During your interview, you'll be making the first person-to-person contact with the company you wish to work for. Use the name of the person interviewing you. Pay very close attention to what that person says, then *respond* to it. It's during the interview that the rubber meets the road. But don't forget that others will be boning up for their interviews, creating their résumés, trying to get the job that you want. That's why guerrillas take the extra step.

### Step Five: Maintain Your Momentum

Many people will want the job for which you're applying. Many will prepare killer résumés. And many will show up mentally well-armed for their interviews. But only the guerrillas will follow up their interviews with thank-you letters.

Does a simple, short thank-you letter make the difference between getting and not getting the job of your dreams? Not really. But the act of writing it may make the difference. You should write it the moment you complete the interview, so you can mail it and it can be read while you are still fresh in the minds of those who took the time to speak with you. In fact, you should bring the stamps and stationery with you and mail the notes from the mailbox on the corner.

Write a letter to every single person you met with. Mention specific highlights from your interview. Most of all, use this opportunity to reinforce your positioning and to focus on the attitudes that will make you an irresistible hire. Exude enthusiasm, persistence, honesty, energy, and more.

Now, it's time to take the final step in using guerrilla marketing to obtain a job.

## Step Six: Accept the Job and Start All Over Again

This is when you make certain that you'll be getting exactly what you expected, which should be very close to getting exactly what you want. Once you've been offered a job, you have, for the first time, the upper hand in the relationship. Your prospective employer has publicly stated that you are the best person on the planet for this job, and, especially at a large organization, this means several people have signed off on the offer. This group-think can work in your favor, as no one wants to have to persuade the group that they were wrong.

At this point, you've got three sets of assumptions and data to work with:

1. The assumptions they've made about you, based on your positioning.
2. The tacit agreements made by you and the employer, based on the offered position.
3. The unstated, and as yet unnegotiated, details to work out.

Every guerrilla knows that this is no time to renegotiate a deal. If you set up certain expectations during the job search process ("eager young graduate needs a foot in the door—will work cheap") this is *not* the time to shift gears.

So be consistent with your positioning. This "first date" you're having will set the tone for the rest of your relationship with your employer. You're not done marketing just because you have the job—you need to market yourself all over again, but this time as an employee.

## Guerrilla Marketing Yourself Into a Better Marriage: Application #2

The bride looks magnificent in her white dress. The groom is proud, excited, and handsome. They walk together down the aisle, certain in their hearts that the vows they've just taken—till death do us part—are sincere and genuine.

Months, years, or decades later, they join the ranks of the divorced. We all know the hardships and costs of ending a marriage, and yet more than half the people who get married divorce. That's an astonishingly high number.

What happens? How do people change from being head over heels in love to being so shattered that they have no choice but to leave? How can we know ourselves and our mates so poorly that we're unable to predict if we'll be able to live with this person a few years down the road? Is it that people change so much over time? Or is it that we've lost the ability and desire to market ourselves to our spouses, to work at building a strong, flexible relationship that can blossom and grow?

Some people seem blessed with a wonderful relationship. They have a significant other, a husband, a wife, who completes their circle. They spend precious little time squabbling and seem to have a relationship that gets stronger with time.

What's the secret? Why are some relationships harmonious and strong, while others seem always on the edge of disaster? If you've ever been in the latter kind of relationship, you know how much of your energy and soul it can drain away. Perhaps the single largest loss of productivity in the workplace is trouble at home. Perhaps the single biggest regret people have at the end of their lives is a lack of success in their family life.

Is there a secret? What do these happy couples do that unhappy couples don't? Virtually everyone is happy on their wedding day. If we could find a way to take these happy couples and teach them tools that would allow them to find even greater levels of happiness, the value would be enormous.

The secret is surprisingly simple:

> I CAN CONTROL THE MESSAGES I SEND
> AND MY LIFE WILL BE BETTER FOR IT.

Participants in wonderful relationships think about how they market themselves to each other. A mate is nothing but a lifetime customer, someone who wants to be with you, to work with you, to spend time with you.

We've already spent a lot of time debunking the myth that you should always do what comes naturally and not think about how your actions send powerful silent messages about you.

No place is this desire to "let it all hang out" more dangerous than in a long-term relationship. After all, most of us go into marriage assuming that it's forever, and the temptation to treat our spouse as a person with no choice but to stick it out is significant. Long ago, businesses learned that customers who are ignored and treated with contempt will go elsewhere. Why should marriage be any different?

Have you ever yelled at your best friend? Given your boss

the silent treatment? Argued incessantly with your carpool mates? Probably not. Yet many couples don't hesitate to treat the most important person in their lives worse than their dog.

Remember when you were dating? You spent hours picking out your clothes, made sure the reservations at the restaurant were confirmed, even washed your car before picking up your honey. In short, you cared about presenting yourself. You took great pains to say, "I think you're important. I want you to like me, to like being with me."

Remember that? When was the last time you acted that way?

Every Friday for the last umpteen years, Jay and his wife Pat have climbed into their van and intentionally gotten lost in the hillsides of Northern California. Three hours after leaving home, they pull into some gas station, somewhere, and ask where they can find the nearest great restaurant (being Northern California, that's a surprisingly easy request). They enjoy a sumptuous lunch and then drive home.

What a marvelous ritual! What a great way to demonstrate how important their time together alone is. Jay and Pat figured out a key building block in their relationship, and they guard it jealously.

Is a long ride on Friday exactly what they both want to do every single week? Probably not. Jay might want to recover from a particularly vicious poker game, and Pat might want to read or paint or whatever. But they understand that they've made a commitment to this ritual and to this time together. They understand that by committing to it, by making it a regular event, the high point of their week, they've created a self-fulfilling prophecy. It works.

Guerrilla marketing in a relationship is a simple corollary to our basic rule:

*Take the time to learn what your partner wants,*
*then make sure you do it.*

It's simple, but it's not easy. After a few months, a few years, a few decades, inertia sets in. We want to coast, to rest, to stop building our relationship. Even after we realize that we've neglected the most important customer in our lives, fixing it isn't always easy or natural. Asking what she wants after ten years of marriage is hard to do if you haven't done it since your engagement!

When faced with this barrier, most people hesitate. Our intuitive goal, after all, is to be accepted for who we are right now. To not have to think about personal marketing, about satisfying other people. To have a loving, caring, supportive spouse—without having to give anything in return.

In black and white, here on the page, the previous sentence is clearly nonsense. Marriage *is* work. Marriage is an ongoing sales and marketing process. It's all about working to do for the other person, to make the other person's life better, happier, sweeter. The pleasure we derive from this process is why we got married in the first place: to give, not to take. And this giving is exactly what we mean by marketing.

Earlier, we showed you that the way you act, the way you talk, the way you dress all communicate to other people. You can send a variety of messages—I care, I resent you, I'm busy—and the messages you send go a long way toward determining how your connections develop.

In the pages that follow, we'll outline some communication skills that will help you discover what your spouse really wants. Then we'll help you brainstorm on ways you can deliver the goods. *Note:* We're making some assumptions and indulging in some stereotypes here. We don't know what your marriage is like. We don't know what you and your spouse want. But there's a surprisingly large overlap across couples, and we're trying to help you get started.

## ─────────── Quiz for Spouses ───────────

*Here's a quick quiz (just like the ones you might see in* Cosmo!*) to discover how much you really know about your spouse:*

1. The thing I do that annoys my spouse more than anything else is _____.

2. My spouse's favorite restaurant is _____.

3. If my spouse could change one thing about me, it's _____.

4. We spend _____ hours of focused (no TV!) time together every week.

5. The biggest challenge facing my spouse at work is ____ _____.

6. My spouse's three closest friends are _____, _____, and _____.

7. My spouse's biggest fear is _____

8. If my spouse used six words to describe me, they would be _____, _____, _____, _____, _____, and _____.

9. My spouse's secret dream is to _____ _____.

10. If my spouse had to marry someone else, it would be _____.

─────────────────────────────────────────

Was the quiz easy? Difficult? After all, this is someone you've lived with, slept with, spoken with for years. It's someone you're planning to spend the rest of your life with. Yet you probably know more about some characters on TV than you know about your spouse.

Did your answer to the fourth question surprise you? It's important to understand that an investment of time is going to be critically important to satisfying the desires of your spouse. After all, the "product" you're selling here is you, and if you're not there, your customer isn't getting what he or she ordered!

Communicating with your spouse about these issues isn't necessarily easy. In fact, we believe that the second biggest problem (after a failure to market ourselves to our spouses) is that people don't make it easy for their spouses to market to them. Instead, far too often people lie in wait for the spouse to mess up, a list of inequities engraved in their psyches.

Miss a birthday, make a mess, leave the lid up—the spouse commits a sin and the aggrieved party pounces. It's so much more effective to say what you want in advance.

Our proposal is that you fill out *your* quiz and the two of you sit down and discuss it. After you've learned something about what she wants and needs, she'll probably ask you what you want and need. We're reprinting the quiz in the Appendix—why not ask your spouse to fill it out, too?

Inevitably, you're going to be surprised by what your spouse said about you. Just as he is going to be surprised by what you said about him. We'll make a sizable bet that a stress-relieving conversation will soon follow. You'll both be able to describe exactly what you're looking for, hoping for, and counting on from your relationship.

A key component of most of the marriages we've seen is

that people want to know that their spouse cares. That in our fast-moving, trust-no-one world, there's someone always there, someone we can trust, someone we can count on, someone who cares about us.

Unfortunately, with the pressures we're under, we don't often get chances to demonstrate how much we care. We wait until it's too late to say what's on our mind, to spend the time, or invest the money to establish to our spouse just how important they are to us.

To get you started, here's a list of twenty ways to send the right message. Some of them are straight out of a greeting card, but there's a reason for that—they work.

Remember, if you're doing this to manipulate someone, it's not going to work. If, on the other hand, your goal is to better express the feelings you already have, be prepared for a miracle. Your relationship will change, and if you keep it up, will stay changed forever.

1. *Never talk about your spouse in a negative way to others.* Like we said, habits form fast, and the more you focus on the positive, the more positively you'll feel toward your relationship.

2. *Never talk about your spouse differently when he or she is in the room from when he or she is not.* The trust you develop by always telling the same story, by always being consistent, will help the foundation of your marriage.

3. *Call each other at work, in the middle of the day, for no reason at all.* Start setting patterns of good feedback and positive messages. These don't have to be long, involved conversations, nor do they have to be gooey, sentimental bon mots. A simple, "Hi, I was just thinking about you" goes a long way.

4. *Dress nicely when you're out with your spouse.* Now

nice may be different for everyone. Nice is not necessarily a suit or a dress. Nice is just whatever it takes to make it clear that spending time with your spouse warrants better presentation than just schlumping around.

5. *Watch what you say and the way you say it.* You can communicate through words, but you also communicate in the way you deliver those words. Are you a yeller? How does raising your voice satisfy your objective of communicating with your spouse? Are you a whiner? Try to think about how you talk to your spouse, and be conscious of how that makes her feel.

One of the huge obstacles facing marriages is decoupling the content of a conversation from its delivery. It's so easy to be hurt by language, so easy to create scars that last and last by injuring the other person with your manner.

The next time you realize you're having an argument with your spouse, pull out a tape recorder and record it. You'll notice a few things happen instantly. When faced with the prospect of posterity, both sides will moderate their tones. Second, you'll start to feel somewhat ridiculous and uncomfortable.

After the argument, the two of you should sit down and listen to yourselves. Try to determine which parts of your argument were healthy communication and which were emotional grandstanding, designed to hurt, not to help.

6. *Send greeting cards regularly.* Some people are especially touched by these, and if it's hard for you to be verbal about certain sentiments this is an effective way to say things that are perhaps hard to put down on paper.

7. *Take retreats.* Isolate some time just for the two of you. Go away, take the phone off the hook, sit by the lake. It's one thing to try to squeeze "quality" time together into an hour or two before bed, it's another to have a space of

uninterrupted time to let your thoughts and feelings expand and interact.

8. *Make a big deal out of a birthday.* For Helene's thirtieth, Seth bought Christmas lights several months in advance, then, on the big day, strung them across the house spelling out the number thirty. Everyone in the neighborhood saw what was going on, and it made both Seth and Helene feel special.

Holidays are good times to do something out of the ordinary for your spouse. Take advantage of their inherent special feeling, and spread it to your relationship.

9. *Hug.* Physical contact is important to some people—vital to others. And there's a difference between sexual contact and just plain physical closeness. Hug each other for no reason. Do it often. Demonstrate nonverbally that you enjoy closeness with your spouse.

10. *Do more than your share, but don't say anything about it.* If your goal is to communicate that you care, that your actions are selfless, then keeping score is the surest way to contradict that message. When both of you start working to do more than your share, the air will practically crackle with energy and enthusiasm. By working *for* the relationship, instead of carefully measuring your piece of it, there's no limit to how far you can go.

11. *Be considerate.* Think about what would make your spouse happy. Make the bed. Especially if you rarely do. Close the seat on the toilet. Ask her if she'd like you to wear cologne. Ask him too!

12. *Break some old habits.* Are you in a rut? Have you allowed your relationship to fall into tired patterns and hackneyed routine? Shake it up. Go out for dinner on Tuesday, not Saturday. Make love in the morning instead of at night. Have a party for no reason at all. Insert some energy

into your good-bye kiss in the morning and your annual pilgrimage to see the cousins. Shaking up your daily life lets your partner know in no uncertain terms that you're committed to revamping, rebuilding, and enjoying your relationship.

13. *Skip TV.* Most couples use the television as a decompressor and a distraction. The average American household has the television on from dinnertime until the eleven o'clock news. Don't fool yourself—you're not courting your spouse if you've got *The Brady Bunch* on the TV. When you were dating, you went out—a bar, a bowling alley, maybe a movie. Sitting *next* to someone all night is not the same as being part of his or her life.

14. *Learn how to give a massage.* Take a class and learn how to spend twenty minutes communicating with your spouse using your fingers. There's almost nothing as unselfish as a compassionate massage. If you're lucky, you might even get one in return!

15. *Brag about your spouse.* Find areas of endeavor that your spouse is really good at—then tell your friends, relatives, and even strangers. Everyone wants someone to be proud of him or her, especially a spouse.

16. *Write it down.* Leave a note in a briefcase, the ice cream, or underneath a pillow. It's one thing to communicate a thought verbally. A written compliment, though, reaches a new height. It's permanent and you can hold it in your hand.

17. *Go for a walk.* On a slow walk on a quiet street, you'll find that the two of you can be together at a different pace and on a different plane than when you're stuck in the same positions in the same house, watching the same shows night after night.

18. *Get in shape.* Not only is it nice to be attractive for

your spouse, but the better you feel about yourself, the more positive you'll be in the relationship as a whole.

19. *Every day, find something about your spouse that you like, and then tell him or her about it.* People love positive feedback. It starts a cycle that inevitably leads to reciprocation. If both of you make a point of reminding yourselves how lucky you are, it'll soon seep in.

20. *Smile.* As much as a smile can do between strangers, it does a hundred times more for someone you love. It says, "No matter how bad my day was, or how tired I am, I'm still glad to be with you." And there are few messages that are nicer to receive than that.

## Guerrilla Market Yourself On-Line: Application #3

Since we live on opposite sides of the country, after meeting in California prior to writing *The Guerrilla Marketing Handbook,* our sole communication was via e-mail. Chapters and letters would be transmitted coast to coast until the book was completed. The communicating was so streamlined that the phone wasn't necessary until we met again in New York to celebrate its publication. In other words, our relationship was up close and cyber before it was up close and personal.

While most of what you've read about the on-line revolution is about small businesses or home businesses acting like big ones, the Net offers a wide range of opportunities, from finding a job to finding a spouse.

This section is about creating and maintaining your on-line persona—who you are and what you do on-line determine the messages people pick up about you.

That's where guerrilla marketing comes in. Even though

the factor of your physical appearance has been removed, there are other aspects of your presence on-line that people can see and sense—your words, your tone, your screen name. The Internet is a very powerful tool, and it's getting more and more so every day. It's important to think about how you can use it to your best advantage.

## On-Line Chat Rooms

The media abounds with fairy tale, but true stories of people who first met on-line, then fell in love and got married. The reason these relationships work out is because connecting on-line often can mean connecting in the mind, the spirit, the soul, and the heart. The superficialities of appearance are eliminated. Some people have referred to on-line chat rooms as "the world's greatest dating services."

Few forms of printed communications are as personal as chat rooms. The next closest are handwritten letters, typed letters, and then e-mail. In this revolution, your personality is expressed by the words you say, the way you say them, and your sensitivity to the situation, not to mention to your chatting companions.

The moment you turn on your computer and go on-line, it's like you're visiting another world—the world of cyberspace. It exists here on earth, but it is unlike the earth with which you're familiar. For one thing, the people are protected, if they want to be, by a cloak of anonymity. A now-famous New Yorker cartoon shows two dogs in front of a computer with one dog saying to the other, "On the Internet, nobody knows I'm a dog."

Truth is that on the Internet, the only thing that people have to go by are the words you use and the way you use them. They can't see you—in most cases—so they can't judge you by the way you look, the clothes you wear, your body language, or by many of the other superficial criteria upon which many people base their judgments. They can't even hear you, so unlike the phone, your voice won't help either.

So your words will carry an extra immediacy, an extra power that is bestowed by your invisibility. The written word gains special force in the magnification of on-line communication.

As blind people have extraordinarily acute hearing because they cannot rely on visual stimuli, the words you use on-line take on extraordinary import because that's all that others can use to get to know you. Each word counts more than the same word used in the context of a face-to-face conversation.

You'll use those words in one of three ways: on bulletin board postings where you write a message and respond to the message of others, in e-mail, which is like regular mail but much faster, and in chat situations where you operate in real time with one or more people—smack dab in the center of the here and now.

Let's stop right here for a moment so you can get clear about being on-line and using the Internet. It has hardly anything to do with computers and almost everything to do with people. Think of a telephone conversation. But on the phone, the words are heard, then disappear. On-line, the words are read, then remain on screen, to be reread, and if you want, to be saved, to be printed, to be studied.

We'll start here with a discussion of chat, which is the least businesslike and most personal form of on-line communication. Communicated on-line in real time, in a chat situation, each of your words carries with it a spontaneity, an immediacy not present in mere written words. This im-

mediacy is not present in bulletin board or e-mail communications—solely in chat situations.

The chats can take place in rooms populated by others
or in complete privacy. For this reason, your typing ability
is part of the way you market yourself. If it's sloppy, you'll
be judged sloppy. If it is slow, people won't see you as sharp
or thoughtful, just slow. In all on-line communications, a
good vocabulary, proper grammar, and accurate spelling are
pluses. But in chat situations, spontaneity rises to the fore.
You don't have the time to mull over your words. You must
think them, then type them immediately.

Hesitation, which may be your ally when writing an e-
mail letter or posting a message, is your enemy when chatting. The last thing people want to do is to say something
on-line then wait for what seems like ages before getting a
response. So if you're a poor typist, we advise that you steer
clear of chat rooms until you pick up those typing skills. As
the Internet grows at a dizzying pace, typing skills become
increasingly important. Not being able to type in the
twenty-first century will be equivalent to not being able to
write in the twentieth.

But even more important than typing ability is writing
ability. If you've got it, you'll be able to establish momentum rapidly in cyberspace. If you don't, guerrilla marketing
yourself on-line will be an uphill battle. Your writing should
be concise, clear, correct, and warm. You've got to know
how to use the language and to spell its words properly.
Poor grammar and poor spelling will have a devastating
effect on your on-line credibility. A wide vocabulary en-
hances it.

A sense of humor will aid your cause, whatever your
cause may be.

Where does guerrilla marketing yourself begin on-line? It

begins with your screen name—usually a name of ten letters or less. In a business setting, companies usually require some combination of first and last names. But on your own, you can pick just about anything that's not taken. Sort of like a personalized license plate.

Jay's screen name is Jayview. Seth's is Sethwood. Both of those names are easy to spell and, just as important, they're easy to remember.

When you sign up for an on-line account, in most cases you get to create your own screen name. Some networks assign you a name that is composed of numbers only. Guerrillas avoid those networks and opt instead for one that gives them the freedom to create a screen name that communicates either their gender, their business, and/or possibly their hobby. Examples of these are Netlady, InsureYou, and Flyingboy. Note that you've been given a chance to position yourself—to pick one word that is, in essence, your brand name.

Of the screen names currently in use, we'd estimate that about one-quarter of them are excellent names, one-quarter are pretty good names, and half are simply terrible—for marketing yourself. It's much easier to relate to someone with a screen name of KathyCan than one with a screen name of TCG098087.

One of the most important needs for human beings is to have an identity. We all have one. But we have a different one on-line. No physical trappings influence it. It comes about from a combination of guerrilla on-line marketing weapons, the most important being your on-line personality.

You shine when you ask questions. You shine when you give intelligent responses to them. You shine when you pay attention to others and don't toot your own cyberhorn. You shine when you can use ordinary words in extraordinary ways, when you can express ideas concisely, when you can get into the flow of an on-line conversation.

Suppose you discover a chat room where the people are discussing your field of expertise—solar energy for homes. Do you announce that your field is solar energy? Not yet you don't. You listen. You contribute to the flow without interrupting it. You pick up, with your attentive reading and listening, that you may be able to help, for example, two of the people in the room.

Anything you say to them in a group situation would be too blatant for most guerrillas. So you should say your piece in a private message, known on America Online as an "Instant Message." Or you can e-mail the people, because you know their screen names and e-mail addresses, and say something to create a relationship.

Although guerrillas recognize that the on-line world is a fertile ground for new customers (or new friends), they never push themselves upon prospects and certainly not upon groups. They prove their expertise by what they say about the topic, not what they say about themselves.

Some on-line services, such as America On-line, allow you to create a profile about yourself. In it, you can give your screen name, real name, location, birthdate, sex, computer used, hobbies, occupation, and a quote that summarizes your essence. Actually, it can be any quote you'd like, but whether you know it or not, it does summarize the essence of you for those profile-readers who have little else to go upon. What you say in that profile markets you as whatever you want to be. Many people don't even enter their profile, so enamored are they of their precious anonymity.

Guerrillas realize that it is a glorious opportunity to put their identity into writing, to market themselves, to create the basis for relationships, to establish the momentum that will help them get what they deserve.

Naturally, you should observe the proper rules of etiquette when venturing into cyberspace. In fact, there's a book, *Netiquette,* by Virginia Shea, that already lays downs the rules of the superhighway.

Essentially it's all common sense, along with a few pointers for the on-line world such as reading the "frequently asked questions" section of anything on-line so that you don't ask stupid questions that have already been addressed and dismissed.

Many on-line relationships are the results of several types of on-line communication—meeting because of a posted message, e-mailing each other, meeting in a chat situation— all mixed together and eventually enriched by a phone conversation or two, then, if necessary, an in-person meeting.

When you are chatting with people in real time on-line, every mistake you make will be read, reread, studied, then possibly saved. You don't have the luxury of saying, "I didn't say that." There it is in black and white. You did say it.

But if you say brilliant things, make witty observations, win hearts with your words, those words will also be read, reread, studied, and possibly saved. They may even be shared with others. So when you're on-line, marketing yourself becomes focused upon the words you say.

### On to E-mail

Chris Locke is perhaps one of the best examples of successful e-mail Guerrilla Marketing. Using nothing but an ever-growing e-mail list, he marketed himself into a succession of great jobs and has built relationships with editors, executives, and power brokers worldwide.

How does he do it? By assiduously building a list of contacts and hand feeding it. He never sends e-mail that the recipient wouldn't want to receive. He always looks for interesting tidbits to forward to people. Most important, he follows the cardinal rule of marketing himself on-line:

*Do for others before you ask them to do for you.*

It's so easy to get on-line, so easy to scam people, so easy to disappear that most people are hesitant about trusting someone they meet in cyberspace. The single best way to get around this problem is never to ask someone to do something for you. That's right. Instead, focus on doing things for other people. Keep doing them. Sooner or later, some of them will repay the favor. Guerrillas have long known that the more you give, the more you get.

This is a conceptual leap that takes time to understand. Hang out on-line, though, and you'll see it in action. Watch a bulletin board, for example, and you'll see one person post a note and ten people answer it. Wow. Those ten guerrillas expect nothing in return. They're volunteering their expertise on parenting or solar energy or venture capital just to help each other. They know, deep in their souls, that when they need help, the community will be there for them.

### Intranets
If you work in a company with internal e-mail, you're dealing with a huge challenge and a huge opportunity. How do you market yourself to the organization with e-mail?

Internal e-mail is extraordinarily powerful. With one click, you can send a message to everyone—straight to the top if you like. You've been handed a very loud megaphone, and you have to determine how to use it to your organization's (and your) best advantage.

Here are nine simple principles that will position you as a thoughtful, constructive employee, someone who's on his way up. While these tips are optimized for *internal* communication, they also work when you're dealing with the outside world:

1. *Don't send copies of your correspondence to strangers.* If you're having a heated back-and-forth with Jeff in purchasing, don't start sending copies of your notes to your boss (whom Jeff doesn't know) without Jeff acknowledging that it's okay. Otherwise, you're putting Jeff on the spot and making your correspondence more public than he's prepared for. The tenor of your e-mail correspondence will change and you'll accomplish less.

2. *Don't blind copy e-mail unless you're prepared to pay the consequences.* Blind copying is a technique in which you send copies of mail to other people secretly. While this is a great way to cover yourself, sooner or later someone will discover the habit and you'll appear deceitful.

3. *Be careful about sending mail to too many people at once.* E-mail is a great tool to let a lot of people know what you're up to. Unfortunately, if you overuse it, you become the girl who cried "wolf" and your mail probably will soon be ignored.

4. *Don't skip too many levels.* While more and more organizations are getting unbureaucratic, most still don't want you to send mail to the president when you're still working in the mailroom. The obvious exception is your boss's boss. If you can naturally and smoothly work her into your correspondence circle, you will end up with far

more exposure in the organization, allowing you to market yourself to your customer's customer—a great place to be.

5. *Offer assistance.* E-mail is an easy way for you to help others in the organization by sharing information and offering advice, contacts, and support. Make it clear in your e-mail that you're a quick, risk-free source, and you'll be able to market yourself to your peers as a leader.

6. *Be careful.* Remember, your e-mail isn't private. Corporations have the right to read the mail their employees send. Servers save copies. Mail gets misdelivered. One employee of Seth's found her way out of a job when she wrote a nasty note about another employee and accidentally sent it to the *subject* of the letter instead of the desired recipient.

No guerrilla would ever e-mail anything he'd be embarrassed to say in public.

7. *Ask for help.* People are eager to pitch in, and it's a great way to start a relationship.

8. *Follow up.* While some correspondences seem to last forever because no one wants to end the "hit reply" sequence, all too often we forget to say thanks for the information provided.

9. *Make a tickler file.* Remember birthdays and upcoming presentations or events. It's easy to press a button and ask how it went, and your thoughtfulness will come through.

# CHAPTER SEVEN
## *The Mirror*

◆

Here's the thing: You can read this entire book and not see yourself. You can study the principles behind guerrilla marketing and still not realize that the tactics you're using are sabotaging you.

Back to marketing again. If the principles of marketing in the business world are clear and easily measured, why is there so much bad advertising? Why are nine dollars out of every ten wasted? For instance, there's a full-page ad for a computer add-on board. The ad is illustrated by a full-page photo of an Olympic diver. Nowhere in the copy is there any connection of the product to the diver. No headline, no reference whatsoever. Did the person who designed the ad realize that the connection between the picture and the product wasn't clear? The advertiser spent more than $20,000 on an ad that's bound to fail. And most marketers who saw the ad knew that right away.

Yet we often make the same kind of mistakes in our personal lives. We can look at someone else, anyone else, and pretty quickly analyze what they're doing wrong. We notice close talkers, bad breath, cheap suits, and people who don't keep their promises. We feel sorry for friends who just can't seem to get it together long enough to land a job. Yet the very next day, we commit sins at least as bad.

Why? Our theory is that in order to live with ourselves, we fool our conscious minds into accepting certain elements of our personality. We fall in love with our own quirks, learning to live with the personal marketing tactics that are costing us so much.

Talk to someone with an obvious self-destructive tendency—someone who's always interrupting or insulting his boss or treating his wife without respect—and the answer will usually be the same, "Oh, I know. But that's just the way I am."

If you've made it this far in the book and haven't had several "aha" moments, you're probably suffering from a broken mirror. You've lost the ability to look at yourself objectively, to independently analyze what works and what doesn't.

We don't believe that you're stuck with the behavior patterns you've learned over the years. Deep down, you have the talent, the desire, and the skills to achieve all the success you deserve. Learning new patterns may be hard, but it's not impossible.

## Ten Hard Questions

The next time you feel that you've failed at something you deserved, ask yourself these ten hard questions. Even better, ask someone you trust. Let's hope that they'll help you identify just what you're doing that's leading to less than satisfactory results.

   1. *Do I know what the person wanted?* Can you write

down in ten words or less what the person was looking for from you?

2. *Did I match his or her expectations?* Did your behavior match your answer to the first question? If you believe it did, then you've likely misjudged the person's objectives, misjudged your behavior, or done something else to lose his or her trust.

3. *Was I marketing myself as trustworthy?* The single largest contributor to most decisions is trust. If you've done something to lose that trust, especially at the beginning of a relationship, it's very difficult to regain it.

4. *Did I keep* all *of my promises?* Even the promises you didn't overtly make. If the other person assumes you've made a promise, then you have.

5. *Did I listen carefully to the person?* Do you *really* understand what you were asked for? This is probably the easiest trap to fall into. Take a few moments to repeat to your prospect exactly what you think he or she is looking for.

6. *Did I hinder my purpose in any way?* Fear of success can drive people to behavior that helps them avoid stressful situations.

7. *Did I talk about myself too much?* You're the second most important person in the room. Don't forget to focus on the other person!

8. *Did I appear nervous or ill at ease?* Trust comes from confidence. If you project nervousness instead, you'll transfer some of that nervousness to the person you're with.

9. *Did I exhibit enthusiasm?* If nervousness dampens trust, enthusiasm builds it. Your excitement is contagious.

10. *Did I fail to follow up on anything?* Remember, guerrilla marketing is a process, not an event. Persist and you will eventually succeed.

## A New Mirror

We believe that your friends will not tell you the truth about you. We're certain that you won't tell yourself the truth (unless cornered). So how do you find out how you're doing? How do you evaluate your success factors and discover the habits that are keeping you from your goals?

The steps that follow are not for the faint of heart. Most of you will ignore them. But if you do, you'll be missing a chance to change your life radically, to discover what you need to do to get what you deserve.

It's scary, but it's worth it.

Start a guerrilla mastermind group. A group of four or six loosely affiliated people who serve no group purpose except to give each other honest marketing feedback.

You're not the only person who needs objective personal marketing feedback. No doubt your colleagues, friends, and coworkers would like some as well.

Start small. Walk into your bank in your business clothes and ask for the manager. Bring a copy of this book with you, and ask her to read this page. Make sure she has a spare minute, and be sure she knows that you're not about to show her a holdup note!

---

Friend,

I'm working to become more aware of the signals I send to those I meet. My appearance, posture, clothes, demeanor, body language, and eye contact are important parts of the way I market myself.

Unfortunately, my friends and coworkers will never give me a straight answer. They have too much to lose and very little to gain by telling me the truth about the impression I make. So my hope is that you, as a respected member of the community, but a disinterested outsider, will take a few minutes to tell me what you think.

To make it easy for you, here are eight areas in which I'd like your feedback. Please compare me to other people who _____ in this community. On a scale of 1 to 10 (10 is the most desirable) how would you rate my:

1. clothes
2. handshake
3. eye contact
4. body language
5. manner of speech/accent
6. breath odor (if any)
7. body odor (if any)
8. demeanor

Thanks!

---

Once you've been through this ordeal with a semi-stranger, find a few compatriots who might be interested in this book. Spread a few copies around (can't blame us for trying to sell a few books!) and meet once a month for lunch to review each other.

Talk about your goals, your strategies, your job searches, your relationships, and tactics you might use to improve your marketing.

If you're having trouble finding people, why not go on-line? We've set up a registry at our web page, as well as a news group, alt.gmy. You can subscribe to the free *Guerrilla Marketing Yourself* newsletter by sending a blank e-mail to GMY@yoyo.com.

# 50 Important Concepts

◆

Iт's IMPORTANT TO IMPLEMENT THE CONTENTS OF THIS BOOK as a system, not piecemeal. By creating and using our information as a plan, you'll find far more success.

To make it easier for you, we've listed the fifty most important concepts here for you, together with a brief summary of each.

1. This book will help you build relationships, get a job, and be treated with respect.
2. Guerrilla Marketing Yourself is about the messages you send, who you send them to, and how you send them.
3. Marketing yourself does not mean being phony. It means doing things intentionally instead of merely reacting.
4. The first step in finding out the messages you send is to describe yourself as a friend would.
5. Don't use these tools to manipulate. If the intentional messages you send don't gel with the person you'd like to be, you'll fail.

6. People judge you. Get used to it.

7. Clutter gives people no other choice but to judge you.

8. Everyone has prejudices. What are yours?

9. Find a mirror—see yourself the way others see you.

10. You have a choice.

11. Marketing is the science of communicating benefits to people so that they'll try what you have to offer—and then delivering on that message to make them happy.

12. Classic marketing is about large budgets, large audiences, and the masses.

13. Guerrilla marketing is the science of marketing to one person at a time.

14. Sales is not marketing and marketing is not sales.

15. Marketing yourself is the most overlooked way to improve your life dramatically. It's not about being phony. It's about communicating.

16. The Golden Secret: I CAN CONTROL THE MESSAGES I SEND AND MY LIFE WILL BE BETTER FOR IT.

17. You can be intentional in your communication by sending messages on purpose.

18. We all have an accidental self and an intentional self.

19. Indulging your reactive, accidental self isn't being "honest." It's merely a lazy way to go through life.

20. You may be sabotaging yourself by sending self-defeating messages.

21. You deserve to be successful. You will be successful as soon as you stop sabotaging your chances at success.

22. Every marketing choice involves a trade-off.

23. Before you market yourself, you must identify your customers.

24. Clutter is the noise you must overcome to send a

message. (Did you notice that we also listed this as #7? That's because you were so busy that we needed to say it twice!)

25. Pigeonholes are the way people quickly force you into one spot in their minds.

26. Positioning is your effort to pick your own pigeonhole.

27. Features are parts of a product or service that people like.

28. Benefits are what customers get out of a feature.

29. A marketing campaign without goals usually fails.

30. You can't be everything to everyone. A general position is no position at all.

31. Your appearance is crucial to your personal marketing.

32. You can fit in or stand out. Up to you.

33. Eye contact and body language are the primeval ways we use to communicate confidence, fear, and power.

34. Unconscious habits allow people to judge you.

35. What you say counts. How you say it counts a lot, too.

36. Everything about your written communication—from stamps to handwriting to paper—sends a message.

37. Expressing your goals in public positions you as well.

38. Your attitude says an awful lot about you.

39. Being ethical is an essential part of Guerrilla Marketing Yourself.

40. What other people say about you counts for even more than what you say about yourself.

41. Everything you say, do, write, and communicate sends a message. Take an inventory of every element of your marketing package and evaluate it.

42. Don't underestimate the telephone. In a medium

where there's nothing but voice, you need to focus even more energy on the tone element.

43. The ten best ways to build positive word of mouth are the following: keeping promises, punctuality, ethics, positive demeanor, respect, gratitude, sincerity, positive feedback, enthusiasm, and initiative.

44. By following the Twelve Rules of Guerrilla Marketing, you can create a program that is guaranteed to work.

45. There are Ten Hard Questions you can ask yourself when your plan isn't working.

46. If your program doesn't work, take a hard look at the four warning signs of an ineffective or inconsistent program.

47. Remember the points of the Guerrilla Marketing Credo.

48. Never stop looking in The Mirror.

49. Find objective people who can provide a new reflection of how you're doing.

50. Guerrilla Marketing Yourself is not a group of separate tools—it's a system. Put the tools together and you're on your way to *getting what you deserve.*

# Workbook for a Guerrilla Marketing Yourself Plan

◆

―――――― **So What's Your Position?** ――――――

Circle the six things that stand out the most about you from these thermometers:

attractive ............unattractive
brilliant...............dim
calculating ..........emotional
caring ................cold
classy .................brassy
competent...........incompetent
cultured .............coarse
driven ................passive
easygoing............fussy
enthusiastic.........bored
ethical................immoral
experienced.........novice
fascinating ..........boring

fast .....................slow
helping................needy
giving..................selfish
honest.................dishonest
intellectual .........down-to-earth
kind ....................cruel
mature ................immature
outgoing .............shy
patient ................impatient
rational...............emotional
secure .................insecure
smart ..................unintelligent
smiling................sour
sultry ..................cold
superficial ..........deep
tardy...................prompt

Write out those six adjectives:

I am _____, _____, _____,

_____, _____, and _____.

This is your current position!

## Features and Benefits Worksheet

WHAT ARE YOUR FEATURES AND BENEFITS?

*Feature*                    *Benefit*

_____        _____

_____        _____

_____        _____

_____        _____

_____        _____

SETTING GOALS

Write down the three things you'd like to achieve or improve over the next 90 days:

1. _____

_____

2. _____

_____

3. _____

_____

_____

——————— **The Twelve Rules of Guerrilla Marketing** ———————

1. BE COMMITTED TO YOUR MARKETING PROGRAM.

I commit to my plan and my positioning statement. Here's what I stand for:

_____

_____

_____

_____

_____

_____

Signed:

_____

2. THINK OF YOUR PROGRAM AS AN INVESTMENT.

Make a list of the education, skills, tools, and background you will need—and what it will cost you in time and money:

| *What You Need* | *What It Will Cost* |
|---|---|
| _____ | _____ |
| _____ | _____ |
| _____ | _____ |
| _____ | _____ |
| _____ | _____ |
| _____ | _____ |

### 3. SEE TO IT THAT YOUR PROGRAM IS CONSISTENT.

Write your message here, so someone can keep tabs on how you're doing.

_____

_____

_____

_____

_____

### 4. MAKE YOUR PROSPECTS CONFIDENT IN YOU.

Make a list of ten things you can do to project (and feel) confidence:

1 _____
2. _____
3. _____
4. _____
5. _____
6. _____
7. _____
8. _____
9. _____
10. _____

### 5. BE PATIENT.

Make a list of five areas or times in your life in which you would have succeeded if you'd just been a little more patient:

1. _____
2. _____
3. _____
4. _____
5. _____

## 6. See Marketing as an Assortment of Weapons.

Write down five weapons or tools you could implement to improve your marketing campaign:

1. _____
2. _____
3. _____
4. _____
5. _____

## 7. Know That Success Comes Subsequent to Making a Good First Impression.

List five things you could do to improve the first impression you make:

1. _____
2. _____
3. _____
4. _____
5. _____

## 8. Make Dealing with You Convenient.

Other than being pleasant and punctual, what five attributes can make you more convenient to work with and be around?

1. _____
2. _____
3. _____
4. _____
5. _____

9. PUT AN ELEMENT OF AMAZEMENT IN YOUR MARKETING.

Make a list of five things that an ordinary person can do to stand out in the "amazing" category:

1. _____
2. _____
3. _____
4. _____
5. _____

10. USE MEASUREMENT TO JUDGE YOUR WEAPONRY.

Make a list of five things you really ought to measure but have been afraid to:

1. _____
2. _____
3. _____
4. _____
5. _____

11. ESTABLISH INVOLVEMENT WITH PEOPLE SO
THEY'LL BE INVOLVED WITH YOU.

Of all the family members you know, which ones do you really care about? How do you show it?

1. _____
2. _____
3. _____
4. _____
5. _____

12. BE DEPENDENT ON OTHERS TO HELP YOU.
THE INTERACTION WILL BENEFIT EVERYONE.

What are some of the ways you've been hurt by something someone has said about you? What are some of the ways you've been helped?

*Hurt*                          *Helped*

_____         _____
_____         _____
_____         _____
_____         _____
_____         _____

―――――――――――――――― **Quiz for Spouses** ――――――――――――――――

*Here's a quick quiz (just like the ones you might see in* Cosmo!*)*
*to discover how much you really know about your spouse:*

1. The thing I do that annoys my spouse more than anything
   else is _____.

2. My spouse's favorite restaurant is _____.

3. If my spouse could change one thing about me,
   it's _____.

4. We spend _____ hours of focused (no TV!) time
   together every week.

5. The biggest challenge facing my spouse at work is _____
   _____.

6. My spouse's three closest friends are _____,
   _____, and _____.

7. My spouse's biggest fear is _____.

8. If my spouse used six words to describe me, they would
   be _____, _____, _____, _____, _____,
   and _____.

9. My spouse's secret dream is to _____
   _____.

10. If my spouse had to marry someone else, it would
    be _____.

—————————— **Your Marketing Plan** ——————————

*Position*
  I am:

  _____

  _____

  _____

  _____

*Goals*
  Over the next three months, I plan to:

  _____

  _____

  _____

  _____

*Measurement*
  I will know whether or not I have achieved my goals when:

  _____

  _____

  _____

  _____

## Your Marketing Plan

### Position

I am:

_____

_____

_____

_____

### Goals

Over the next three months, I plan to:

_____

_____

_____

_____

### Measurement

I will know whether or not I have achieved my goals when:

_____

_____

_____

_____

———————————— **Your Marketing Plan** ————————————

## *Position*
I am:

_____

_____

_____

_____

## *Goals*
Over the next three months, I plan to:

_____

_____

_____

_____

## *Measurement*
I will know whether or not I have achieved my goals when:

_____

_____

_____

_____

―――――――――――――― **Your Marketing Plan** ――――――――――

## *Position*
I am:

_____

_____

_____

_____

## *Goals*
Over the next three months, I plan to:

_____

_____

_____

_____

## *Measurement*
I will know whether or not I have achieved my goals when:

_____

_____

_____

_____

# INDEX

# Our Promise and Our Guarantee

We promise we won't ask you to manipulate anyone. The guerrilla marketing methodology is based on delivering on your promises. Marketing yourself for success works as long as you follow through and deliver.

Here's our guarantee; we're dead serious about it, so hold us to it if the plan doesn't work: Give the concepts in **Get What You Deserve!** sixty days. Write them down, keep track of the changes you make in your behavior, your actions, your goals. If you don't notice a significant change within two months, send us this book, your receipt, and a letter outlining what you did, and we'll gladly refund your money. This offer is made solely by the authors. Do *not* return material to either the bookstore or the publisher. All proof-of-purchase must be sent to SGP, 1 Bridge Street, Suite 26, Irvington, NY 10533. Offer valid through August 31, 1998.